Discovering Christ In Philippians

Discovering Christ

In Philippians

Donald S. Fortner

Go *publications*

Go Publications
3 South Parade, Seascale, Cumbria, CA20 1PZ, ENGLAND.

ISBN 978-1-908475-23-7

This book is dedicated,
— as an expression of my deep appreciation —
to

Those many pastors, churches, and friends far and wide who have been so thoughtful and caring of me since the Lord took my dear husband home. It was Don's desire that I try to get as much as possible of his unpublished works in print before the Lord takes me home.

I would also like to express my special appreciation to Evelyn Wang and Larry Criss who helped me in proof reading this manuscript and to Peter Meney for his assistance in making *Discovering Christ in Philippians* a reality.

Shelby Fortner

Table of Contents

Foreword

It is both a privilege and honour for me to write the foreword to this book by my dear friend and pastor Don Fortner. This book, as with all Don's writings, points us to the Lord Jesus Christ. This commentary reminds us there is no understanding of the word of God if we fail to see Christ in it. If our reading of this epistle to the Philippians does not bring us to a fresh discovery of Jesus Christ, we have taken a wrong turn.

Just as Paul instructed those believers at Philippi, Don reminds us as well, we always have reason to rejoice. If we have Christ, if we are washed in his blood and robed in his perfect righteousness we have that which the world did not give and can never take from us. And even though the child of God in this world suffers as other men do, and in ways that the lost man cannot, we still have the joy of knowing whom we have believed.

In reading *Discovering Christ In Philippians*, we are constantly encouraged to press on toward the mark for the prize of the high calling of God in Christ Jesus. My good friend Don Fortner has finished his race and now realizes the unspeakable joy of being forever with the Lord. I can only imagine Don's delight in now beholding the face of his Redeemer, the Lord Jesus Christ. The One whose gospel he so long faithfully preached he is now in the presence of.

In chapter 10 of this book, Don writes, 'When I am gone, and my work is ended, I hope I will have contributed something to the spiritual good of my generation for the glory of God. This is my life's task.'

I believe Don has done that very thing many times over, and this book is another example of it. May God be pleased to use this work for his own glory, and may we who read it be helped by His Spirit to discover the Lord Jesus Christ, and the riches of his grace to needy sinners.

Pastor Larry Criss,
Fairmont Grace Church,
Sylacauga, Alabama

Introduction

The church at Philippi was very dear to Paul. He looked upon these men and women as his children in the faith. He had begotten them by the gospel. Paul had been called to preach the gospel to them in a very unusual way. A vision appeared to him in the night, and 'There stood a man of Macedonia, and prayed him, saying, Come over into Macedonia, and help us' (Acts 16:9).

Paul was only at Philippi for a short time. While he was there he suffered many things and was thrown into prison. But during his brief stay, Lydia and the Philippian jailor were converted, along with many from their respective households. From this small beginning, the church at Philippi had now grown into a large and flourishing congregation.

The believers at Philippi heard that Paul was suffering in prison in Rome. These dear saints took up an offering for him and sent their pastor, Epaphroditus, to visit him. Epaphroditus and Paul had a good visit together; and when Epaphroditus started to leave, Paul sent this letter by him to the saints of God at Philippi. In the letter he expresses his love and gratitude toward the people of God and gives them some account of his bonds and afflictions for the gospel's sake, assuring his friends that the hand of God had made even these things useful to him.

In this epistle, Paul takes the opportunity to minister to the people of God at Philippi and to encourage them to faithfully endure their trials, afflictions, and persecutions for the glory of Christ. He admonished them to cultivate love, and unity, and peace among themselves. And he warned them to beware of those false teachers, who were the enemies of the cross of Christ. Even in those days there were many who tried to

11

mix Christ and Moses, the gospel and the law, grace and works. Paul was gravely concerned that the saints of God at Philippi might be influenced by the evil influence of such teachers.

As in Paul's day, so it is today. Among preachers and teachers there are some who are 'the enemies of the cross of Christ'. The vast majority of people are religious. Most profess religion of one sort or another and we may well say there has never been so much religion in the world as there is at this present time, be it Christianity or something else. Religion has become very popular. The biggest business in America is 'Big Business Religion'. Preachers are found on every street corner. Our radios and televisions broadcast religion twenty-four hours a day. Some are truly God's servants, but most are not. A very important question arises, a question which should be of great concern to us all. Who are the servants of Christ? The Apostle John tells us, 'Beloved, believe not every spirit, but try the spirits whether they are of God: because many false prophets are gone out into the world' (1 John 4:1).

I know this, – those who are truly the servants of Jesus Christ are men whom God has set apart and chosen for the work of the gospel. They are called and sent of God. The servants of Jesus Christ are men whom God himself has put into the ministry. If God puts a man into the ministry, several things will be evident:

1. He will put his grace in that man's heart. Those who are called of God to the work of the gospel know and love the Lord Jesus Christ.

2. He will give him the message of the gospel. No man is called of God who does not know and preach the gospel, the gospel of substitutionary redemption, the gospel of God's free and sovereign grace in Christ.

3. He will give him the gifts of the ministry. If a man is called of God to preach the gospel, he can preach! He has the ability to teach others, to communicate and instruct others in the gospel.

4. He will give him a place to preach. 'A man's gift maketh room for him' (Proverbs 18:16). If God has called a man to preach the gospel, the people of God will give him their attention. Someone will want to hear him.

5. He will give that man a genuine love and concern for the people of God. His desire to preach will not be for personal

ambition, for gain, or for position. It will be his desire to serve the people of God. This is what Paul said, 'We preach not ourselves, but Christ Jesus the Lord; and ourselves your servants for Jesus' sake' (2 Corinthians 4:5).

This is what I want you to see, the servants of Jesus Christ are men whose hearts are devoted to the people of God. Our concern is not for ourselves, but for the glory of God. Our dedication is not to ourselves, but to the gospel of the grace of God. We are devoted not to our own welfare, but to the welfare of the people of God.

The greatest blessing God can give to any man, to any church, or to any community is for him to send one of his servants to preach the gospel among them. The greatest blessing God can ever give you is for him to send to you one of his pastors, one of the servants of Jesus Christ (Jeremiah 3:15).

Chapter 1

'The Servants Of Jesus Christ'

Paul and Timotheus, the servants of Jesus Christ, to all the saints in Christ Jesus which are at Philippi, with the bishops and deacons: Grace be unto you, and peace, from God our Father, and from the Lord Jesus Christ. I thank my God upon every remembrance of you. Always in every prayer of mine for you all making request with joy, For your fellowship in the gospel from the first day until now; Being confident of this very thing, that he which hath begun a good work in you will perform it until the day of Jesus Christ: ... That ye may approve things that are excellent; that ye may be sincere and without offence till the day of Christ; Being filled with the fruits of righteousness, which are by Jesus Christ, unto the glory and praise of God.

(Philippians 1:1-11)

In these opening eleven verses of his letter the Apostle Paul sets before us five characteristics by which you may know those who are the true servants of the Lord Jesus Christ.

1. They know their position and responsibilities (v. 1)

If a man is called of God to the work of the gospel, if God puts him into the ministry, he will not need any strings upon him. He knows his position. He knows what his work is, and he willingly performs it.

Paul speaks of himself and Timothy as the servants of Jesus Christ. Paul was an apostle. Timothy was only a young pastor. But both were the servants of Christ, willingly enslaved to the service of Christ. They supported and honoured one another (Philippians 2:19-22). They were both given for the same purpose and dedicated to the same object (Ephesians 4:8-12).

They were not lords, but servants, not reverends, but servants, not fathers, but servants, not doctors, but servants, not pompous, but lowly servants. These men were dedicated and devoted servants of Christ. They lived to serve Christ, to show forth his glory, to preach his gospel, and to serve his church (Acts 15:26; 20:28).

Paul addressed his letter to the whole church at Philippi. Because he was the Lord's servant, ordained as an apostle of Christ, he spoke to the whole assembly with divine authority. Because of this divine authority the whole church was obliged to follow his instruction.

His letter was to the saints: those men and women whom God set apart, or sanctified as his own in election, redemption, and calling.

His letter was to the bishops: the pastors, or elders of the church. While Epaphroditus was the one pastor, whose task it was to oversee the church, rule it and govern it, there were many elders who assisted him in the work. Elders are men who are set apart as spiritual guides and teachers under the pastor. And,

His letter was to the deacons: those men who take care of the physical, financial affairs of the congregation (Acts 6:2-4). Deacons are to relieve the pastor of mundane affairs and routine responsibilities so he can give himself exclusively to the ministry of the Word.

2. They seek the spiritual welfare of God's people (v. 2)
The servants of Christ desire and seek the blessings of the grace of God upon his people. Every true pastor has one primary concern for his congregation, one thing for which he labours, one thing that drives and motivates him. He seeks the spiritual welfare of God's people.

Three things must constantly concern my heart, and the hearts of every true pastor. These three great principles must motivate our actions for they are the purpose of our preaching: first, the glory of God in Christ, second, the furtherance of the gospel of Christ, and third, the eternal welfare of God's elect, chosen people in Christ.

Grace is the saving goodness and power of God toward his people. There can be no peace where there is no grace. Peace comes with the sense, the felt awareness, of divine favour. Peace is the quietness of conscience that comes when grace is established in the heart, peace with God in justification, the peace of God in regeneration, and peace from God among his people. How blessed it is to see the people of God dwelling together in the love, unity, and peace of Christ.

Grace and peace come to us from God the Father through the Lord Jesus Christ, and Christ, as Mediator, is the channel through which all the blessings of God come to his people (Ephesians 1:3, 4).

3. They remember the Lord's people (vv. 3-6)
When I say that God's servants remember the Lord's people, I am saying simply that they always have them in mind. God's people are always on the hearts of his servants. There is never a time when their cares, their trials, their needs, and their burdens are not on the pastor's heart.

Paul remembered the Philippians and carried them on his heart. Though they were far apart, he thought of them continually. He rejoiced to speak of them to others and with great joy heard others speak to him of them. The things which he suffered at Philippi were nothing to him in comparison with the joy he felt when he remembered what God had done in that place.

He remembered the Lord's people in prayer. It was natural for him to pray for them because he carried them on his heart (1 Samuel 12:23, 24). He gave thanks for what the Lord had done among them, giving them fellowship in the gospel. God had graciously preserved them in the faith, and hope, and love of the gospel. The church at Philippi was truly a church, a fellowship of the Lord's people. They were of one heart and one mind in Christ.

He gave thanks for the confidence he had regarding their future (v. 6). As God had begun the good work of grace in them, he would surely bring it to perfection (Psalm 138:8; Isaiah 64:8).

4. They sincerely love the Lord's people (vv. 7, 8)
In these verses Paul expresses the ardent affection he had for the Lord's people at Philippi. He had good reason for loving these people. They had been made partakers of the grace of God. They had stood firm in the defence of the gospel. And they had stood by him, even when others denied him.

17

Paul's love was genuine and sincere. He calls God for witness of the sincerity of his heart-affection for them. His heart greatly longed for them. With the compassion of Christ, he truly loved these people. He seems to say, 'Whether you know it or not, God, who knows my heart, knows that I truly love you and want the best for you.' In his heart he longed for their spiritual welfare.

5. They pray for the Lord's people (vv. 9-11)
In these verses Paul tells the Philippian believers what he desired for them, and how he prayed to God for them. I think I can honestly say as God's servant that these are the very things which I pray for and desire from God for those to whom I minister.

I pray that God will make us a loving people. 'That your love might abound yet more and more.' May God make us to abound in love. In love for Christ and love toward one another (1 Corinthians 13:1-3).

I pray that God will give us knowledge and understanding in the gospel. 'That your love may abound yet more and more in knowledge and in all judgment.' Let us abound in love. But let that love abound in knowledge and in judgment. It is not enough to have strong passions and zeal. We must also have knowledge and understanding (Romans 10:2).

I pray that God will give us spiritual discernment. 'That you may approve things that are excellent', or 'That you may discern things that differ'.

I pray the Lord will give us sincerity of heart and purpose. 'That ye may be sincere.' Oh, that we may be sincere in our worship, sincere in our motives, sincere in our works, and sincere in our devotion to the glory of Christ and the gospel of the grace of God. God save us from pretence and hypocrisy!

I pray that we will be an inoffensive people, 'without offence'. We must not be easily offended. We must not be the cause of offense to any. If men are offended with us, let their offence be over the gospel.

I pray that we might be a fruitful people (v. 11). 'Being filled with the fruits of righteousness.' May we manifest the fruit of the Spirit and be useful in this generation.

In all things, I pray that God our Father and the Lord Jesus Christ our Saviour may be glorified. 'Unto the glory and praise of God.' In all things, let us seek the glory of God (1 Peter 4:11; 1 Corinthians 10:31).

While it is a great blessing of God's grace when he sends one of his servants, it also places men under great responsibility (Hebrews 13:7, 17). Those to whom he is sent have a responsibility to remember to pray for God's servant, to support God's servant, to follow God's servant, and to obey God's servant.

Chapter 2

A Matter Of Confidence

Being confident of this very thing, that he which hath begun a good work in you will perform it until the day of Jesus Christ.

(Philippians 1:6)

There are some things going on in the world around us which should be of concern to us. The horrible things we hear on the news each day are very alarming. Those things are of real concern to me. But I am far more concerned about what I see taking place in the religious world. My warfare is not with flesh and blood, but with spiritual wickedness in high places. We are living in the most perilous, the most spiritually dangerous times this world has ever known. I am concerned for the glory of God, the gospel of God, and the people of God. I know that for the church of the Lord Jesus Christ, these are days of great tribulation, such as the world has never seen (2 Thessalonians 2:3-12; Revelation 20:1-3).

We must face the facts. I know the seriousness of the charges I am about to bring. But I see things going on in the religious world that cause me grave concern. The simple facts we must face are these:

The most prominent, the most powerful, the most popular, the most influential religious leaders of our day are false prophets. They are men who are preaching another gospel. The gospel of this day is man-centred. It talks about salvation that begins and ends with man. It promotes man's dignity, man's power, man's righteousness, man's will, man's rights, man's accomplishments. The gospel of this day, in its essence, is a denial of the character and work of God. It robs God of his sovereignty, his power, his glory, his grace, and his supremacy in salvation.

This false gospel is being universally received by men as the truth of God, while the gospel of God's free-grace in Christ is looked upon as heresy.

Men, women, and children are being deceived by the millions. They are being persuaded to call upon a god who cannot save and their souls are deluded with a false hope in a false god. They have a sense of security, but their security is ill-founded. They have a refuge, but their refuge is a refuge of lies (Isaiah 28:14, 15, 17).

I have seen many who once walked in the truth turned aside, either to apostate religion or to the cares of this world (1 John 2:19).

These facts would make me tremble were it not for this one thing. I know that the ark of the Lord is safe. I am confident that God's cause is not in jeopardy. Those three things about which I am most concerned will not be harmed, or even shaken, by the terrible evil of this day. (1.) The glory of God shall be maintained. (2.) The gospel of God shall accomplish its purpose. And (3.) the people of God shall be saved. My heart is comforted and greatly encouraged by the fact that the perfect, eternal salvation of God's elect is secure and absolutely certain. These things give me peace before God, even in the face of disturbing facts.

This is a matter of confidence. I am fully persuaded that the purpose and work of the Lord our God will be carried on to perfection. 'Being confident of this very thing, that he which hath begun a good work in you will perform it until the day of Jesus Christ.' This is cause for rejoicing; for comfort, confidence, and thanksgiving.

Paul had been favoured with such clear views of the character of God, the work of Jesus Christ, and the power of the Holy Spirit, that he, too, was certain that God would not be frustrated in his purpose or defeated in his work. Paul assures us of five things in Philippians 1:6.

1. Salvation is the good work of grace
Paul speaks of a good work which God had begun in 'all the saints in Christ Jesus which are at Philippi'. He is telling us that salvation is the good work of God's grace. He begins where all gospel truth must begin. He is telling us that salvation is a good work, but his primary point of emphasis is that salvation is God's work.

I remind you that salvation is God's work, and God's work alone. Salvation is not to be attributed to man in any measure or sense whatsoever. It would be well if our modern-day preachers could spend three days with Jonah down in 'Whale-Belly Seminary'. There they would learn that 'salvation is of the Lord' (Jonah 2:9).

Salvation is the co-operative work of God the Father, God the Son, and God the Holy Spirit (Ephesians 1:3-14). God the Father purposed the salvation of his elect. God the Son purchased the salvation of his elect. God the Spirit performs salvation in the elect.

Salvation is a co-operative work, performed by the Three Persons of the Holy Trinity. But salvation is not in any sense a co-operative effort between God and man.

In this passage, Paul is talking about our present experience of salvation. His subject is the work of God upon the hearts of his people by the power and grace of the Holy Spirit. In its very beginning, Paul declares that salvation is the work of God's grace. Salvation does not begin with man; it begins with God. Man does not take the first step, God does. Man is dead in sin. Life must come to him from the Giver of life, or he must forever remain dead (Ephesians 2:1-3).

If ever a person realizes who man is and what his condition is before God, he will be made to acknowledge that if any man is saved, he must be saved by the grace of God. Similarly, if men ever realize what salvation really is, they will surely see that it must be the work of divine grace alone.

There can be one reason only why people speak of salvation as though they could either cause it or prevent it. The simple reason is this: they do not know what salvation is. They have never been taught doctrinally and they have never been taught spiritually.

Salvation is regeneration; the giving of life, it is resurrection; life from the dead, and it is a new creation, so that the Apostle can say 'Therefore if any man be in Christ, he is a new creature: old things are passed away; behold, all things are become new' (2 Corinthians 5:17).

Charles Spurgeon said, 'When Paul declares that the good work was begun by God, I gather that the faintest gracious desire that ultimately blossoms into the fragrant flower of earnest prayer and humble faith, is the work of God.'

Paul also describes salvation as 'a good work'. Salvation is good in its cause. It is the will and good pleasure of God. Salvation is good in itself. It is an illumination of the heart. It is the subduing of the will. It is the implanting of the Divine nature and is the forming of Christ in the soul. Salvation is good in its results. It makes a man an heir of all good. It turns a man from darkness to light. It produces peace in the heart. It purges the conscience and brings glory to God.

2. Salvation is an inward work of grace

Salvation is God's 'good work in you'. Salvation is not an external work, but an internal work. It is not an external reformation of life. It is not an outward lamentation for sin. It is not ceasing from certain forms of evil. It is not submitting to religious customs and practices. Salvation is something within a man. It is a renewing and a renovation of the heart and soul (John 4:24; Romans 10:9, 10; Philippians 3:3). Salvation is a heart work. It is God establishing his law in the heart, in the inward parts of his people (Hebrews 8:10-12; 10:16, 17).

To be saved is to know God; it is to have Christ formed in you. To be saved is to have your heart's affection turned toward Christ, and to submit all things to him. To be saved is to be motivated by the glory of Christ, and to be governed by the principles of love, faith, and righteousness. In a word, salvation is the surrender of the heart to the claims of Christ (Luke 14:25-27, 33).

3. Salvation is a work of grace begun in this life

When is a person saved? That is not an easy question to answer. I have been saved. I am being saved. I shall be saved. But there is a sense in which salvation is only begun here. It is not completed until the day of Jesus Christ. But it is and must be begun. John Gill said that salvation 'may be said to begin as soon as light is let into the soul by the Spirit of God; when it sees its lost estate and its need of a Saviour, for as the first thing in the old creation was light, so it is in the new'.

Salvation is begun when the light of the gospel shines into a person's heart, revealing the light of the glory of God in the face of Jesus Christ. A person is saved when it pleases God. A person is saved when he or she sees the glory of God in the cross of Christ and the guilty soul is able to justify God in its own condemnation. A person is saved when the authority of Christ as Lord is submitted to and the sinner hears and believes the gospel of the grace of God in Christ.

Yet, even when we have come this far, the work of salvation is only begun. It is not yet finished, complete and perfect. Our faith, hope, love, and knowledge are far from being perfect. Sin and corruption still dwell within us.

4. What God has begun he will finish
That which God has begun in us, he will carry on and bring to completion. The Lord is not done with us yet, but he will carry on his work until it is done. Before sin entered the world everything in God's physical creation was perfect and complete. Having destroyed sin forever, everything in God's new, spiritual creation will also be brought to perfection and completion.

Mark it down, every one of those whom God has purposed to save will have his grace bestowed upon them. And every one of those who have grace bestowed upon them will be brought into the perfection of eternal glory. Not one of God's elect shall perish. God will finish what God has begun. The glory of God and the purpose of God demands it. The redemption of Christ and the intercession of Christ demands it. The justice of God demands it.

God will never turn from his purpose. He will never be defeated in his power. He will never be frustrated in his work. Who, or what, is going to prevent Almighty God from doing what he has purposed and promised to do? The very notion is ridiculous.

5. God's eternal purpose of grace will be perfectly accomplished
In the day of Jesus Christ, in the final consummation of all things, God's elect shall stand before him in perfect righteousness. They will, every last one be perfectly, completely saved in body, soul, and spirit (Romans 8:28-39). This is what we are looking forward to. This will be the satisfaction of our hearts and the final end of our salvation (Psalm 16:10, 11; 17:15).

In these days of terrible apostasy and religious deception, my heart is comforted by these facts. These things are so established in my soul and mind by the Spirit of God, that my heart is kept in peace before him. It is a matter of confidence in my soul. The glory of God shall be maintained. The gospel of God shall accomplish its purpose. And the people of God shall be saved. All is safe and secure. The cause of God is in the hands of God.

Would you know this blessed security? Stop looking for hope in yourself. Rest your soul upon Christ alone.

> My name from the palms of His hands
> Eternity will not erase;
> Impressed on His heart it remains
> In marks of indelible grace.
> Yes, I to the end shall endure,
> As sure as the earnest is given;
> More happy, but not more secure,
> The glorified spirits in heaven.

Augustus M. Toplady

Chapter 3

The Four Great Concerns Of My Heart

But I would ye should understand, brethren, that the things which happened unto me have fallen out rather unto the furtherance of the gospel: So that my bonds in Christ are manifest in all the palace, and in all other places; And many of the brethren in the Lord, waxing confident by my bonds, are much more bold to speak the word without fear … Having the same conflict which ye saw in me, and now hear to be in me.

(Philippians 1:12-30)

Like you, as a person living in this world, I have many cares and responsibilities. Like you, I have a family to feed and clothe, a family that needs my love, my time, my care, and my attention. I have a wife who depends upon me to love her, to provide for her, to protect her, and to please her. As a man, and as a believer, I must not neglect these responsibilities. God has given them to me, and it is my privilege to be faithful in these responsibilities for the glory of Christ.

But I must not allow these natural cares and responsibilities to be the pre-eminent concerns of my life. There is nothing in all the world more dangerous to my soul, or to yours, than the cares of this world. There are some things more important than these earthly cares. There are some things for which my personal cares must take a back seat.

I know this, there is nothing we have as the children of God, whether in nature or in grace, that is not the gift of God. Each of us have received particular talents, endowments, and abilities that are physical, material, and spiritual; and we are to use those gifts and blessings as faithful stewards before God. God has given me nothing, even my family, that I might consume it upon my own lust, or use it to provide for my own comfort and satisfaction.

All that God has given to us, he has given so that we might use it in the accomplishment of his purpose, for the glory of his name, and for the good of his people. Our homes, our property, our money, our talents, all that we have and all that we are should be devoted to Christ and used for Christ. The beauty of Christ, the love of Christ, the grace of Christ, the faithfulness of Christ, and the generosity of Christ should be reflected in us.

In Philippians 1:12-30, Paul gives an example of this spirit. Paul was a man who had wilfully and deliberately devoted himself to Christ. He had given himself and all he had to the cause of Christ. He was in prison at Rome only because he faithfully preached the gospel. Even now, when he might have sought comfort, he was ministering to the comfort of others.

The Philippians had heard of Paul's troubles, and were concerned for him. He wrote this letter to give them a true and proper understanding of his trials and afflictions. He wrote so the weak among them might not be offended by his imprisonment, and to encourage them all to bear their afflictions for Christ's sake with patience and cheerfulness. Paul's concern was not for his own comfort and welfare. His concern was for the gospel of Christ, the salvation of his soul, the glory of Christ, and the welfare of God's elect.

Like Paul, each of us should devote ourselves entirely to the cause of Christ. I wish we could say with our Lord, 'The zeal of thine house hath eaten me up'. But, for most of us, honesty would compel us to say, 'The zeal of my house hath eaten me up.' As we go through these verses, I am going to share with you four great concerns of my heart, which were also the concerns of Paul's heart. I trust that God the Holy Spirit will make them the concerns of your heart as well.

Devotion to the gospel of Christ (vv. 12-18)
'I am set for the defence of the gospel.' This is my first concern. I am not devoted to religion. I am not devoted to a denomination. I am not devoted to a system of theology. But I am devoted to the gospel. I am devoted to the gospel of God's sovereign grace, the gospel of

substitutionary redemption, the gospel of satisfactory, effectual atonement, the gospel of almighty, irresistible grace.

I am more consumed by and committed to the preaching of the gospel today than I have ever been in my life. God helping me, I will hold the banner high, and I call upon you to rally around it. By the grace of God, let us be devoted to these two things:

'The furtherance of the gospel.' I am determined to preach the gospel wherever I can, whenever I can, however I can, and to as many people as I can in this generation. I am going to support the gospel and those who faithfully preach it in any way I can. I cannot speak for others, but 'as for me and my house, we will serve the Lord'.

Also, 'I am set for the defence of the gospel'. Let us not silently tolerate any compromise, any toning down, or any perversion of the gospel of God's free and sovereign grace in Christ. The offence of the cross is our glory and our strength.

This is what Paul told the Philippians in verses 12-18. It gave Paul great joy to know that all that had happened to him had been ordained and used of God for the furtherance of the gospel. It is as though he said, 'So what if I am imprisoned; so what if I am made the object of slander and of bondage; all that has happened to me has been used of God for the furtherance of the gospel. Nothing else really matters.' He says as much in Acts 20:24.

His imprisonment actually served to advance and give renewed strength to the preaching of the gospel (v. 12). As a result of Paul's imprisonment, the gospel had become an issue throughout Caesar's court (v. 13; Acts 26:26). And many of his brethren had been inspired by Paul's afflictions to proclaim the gospel more boldly (v. 14).

The greatest joy of Paul's heart was to know that Christ was being preached in all the fulness of his grace and glory (vv. 15-18). Whoever these men were of whom Paul speaks in theses verses, they truly preached the gospel of God's redeeming grace in Christ, or Paul would not have rejoiced in their ministries (Galatians 1:8).

Regretfully, there has always been some strife and division among God's true people, even in the apostolic age. So long as we are in this flesh, such things must be endured. But Paul had enough grace to overlook the faults of his true brethren, so that he truly rejoiced to know that they were preaching Christ. What an example for us!

Some preached Christ of envy and strife. They envied Paul's gifts, his power, and his success. Now that he was in jail, they hoped to gain the honour and applause of the church.

Some preached Christ with a contentious, divisive spirit. Their contention was not over the gospel of substitution, but over words, practices, church government, prophecy, and vain questions about the law. These were men of a party spirit, who hoped to make Paul's chains of imprisonment more bitter.

When Paul preached, he met with trouble, imprisonment, and punishment; but here they were preaching with little difficulty and opposition. Probably, they thought Paul's troubles were of his own making. If he had been more like them, not so bold, not so plain, not so insistent, he might not have had so much trouble.

But there were some who preached Christ with hearts of true, sincere love, love for Christ, love for the church, love for the lost, love for Paul. In any case, Paul rejoiced to know that Christ was preached in the glory of his person, in the fulness of his grace, in the excellency of his righteousness, in the efficacy of his atonement, in the power of his intercession.

There are a good many gospel preachers around the world who, for one reason or another, choose not to associate themselves with each other. Perhaps their personalities conflict. Hopefully, that can be corrected. They may differ in the way they conduct their ministries, or even in minor points of doctrine, which cannot in conscience be surrendered. Sinful men are not infallible! But any man who faithfully preaches the gospel of God's free and sovereign grace in Christ is my brother and friend! I am set only for the defence of the gospel. Nothing else is important! I rejoice that Christ is preached, no matter who the preacher is!

Salvation in Christ (vv. 19, 20)
Second, the great desire and concern of my heart is that in the last days I shall be found in Christ, washed in his blood, robed in his righteousness, and accepted in his Person. Being confident that I shall be saved by the merits of Christ, nothing else really matters. If truly it is well with my soul, all is well! Brother Scott Richardson used to say, 'I have never had any bad news since I got the good news!'

I know all things are being governed by God for my eternal good (v. 19; Romans 8:28). Even that which appears to be, and is intended by man to be evil, is ruled by God for my good (Isaiah 54:17). No evil shall happen to God's elect. With such expectation, hope, and confidence, I will never be ashamed of the gospel, nor of anything that I may suffer for the gospel's sake (v. 20).

The glory of Christ (vv. 20-24)
In the third place, whether I live or die, whether I am in health or in sickness, whether I am highly esteemed or vilely reproached, whether my family and friends understand me and support me or if they become ashamed of me and forsake me, I have one motive, one desire, one concern, one driving ambition to which I am devoted. The one great concern of my heart is 'that Christ shall be magnified in my body'.

I know this, 'For me to live is Christ, and to die is gain'. If I live, it will be for Christ's glory and by Christ's power. He is the Giver of life. He is the Sum and Substance of life. He is the Hope of eternal life. But for me, and for every true believer, to die is gain. When I die, I will gain release from all pain and sorrow. When I die, I will gain release from all trial and temptation. When I die, I will gain release from all sin, and I will gain all the glory and bliss of Christ's eternal presence in heaven.

So far as I am concerned, whatever is best for the glory of Christ and the good of his people, that is what I want. When he is done with me, I shall be happy to lay aside this troublesome, wearisome robe of flesh.

Welfare of God's elect (vv. 25-30)
The fourth great concern of my heart is for the welfare of God's elect. The church of God is my family. The people of God, these are my mother and father, wife and daughter, my brothers and sisters (Matthew 12:46-50).

Paul told the Philippians that he was confident he would live a while longer on the earth to preach the gospel to them that they might grow in grace and in the 'joy of faith' (v. 25). Paul knew that where there is a true, saving knowledge of God in the heart, there will also be joy in the heart. This is a peaceful satisfaction, the contentment, and calm of the heart that is produced by faith in Christ. It is a calm resignation to the will of God, the way of his providence, and the wisdom of his works.

And there is nothing that increases the believer's joy like a fresh revelation of Christ, of his Person, his love, his grace, and his work.

So long as he lived, Paul was determined he would give himself to the work of the gospel, devoting his time and talents to the welfare of God's people (v. 26). Though he was in prison, he found a way to serve the church of God, for the glory of Christ.

In verses 27-30, Paul admonished the church at Philippi to seek the honour of Christ in all things, and I give these admonitions to you for Christ's sake. Let us conduct ourselves at all times, and in all things, in a manner which is becoming to the gospel of Christ (v. 27). Let us live, and walk, and talk as men and women who follow Christ in the church, at home, at work, in business, and in our personal behaviour. Let us strive together with one mind and one heart for the faith of the gospel.

Do not be afraid of our enemies (v. 28). The fact that men oppose us for the sake of the gospel is evidence of their condemnation and of our salvation. Our trials, whatever they are, are ordained of God, so we should bear them in faith, patiently (v. 29). Whatever God has ordained for us is good for us.

Children of God, we are all in the same battle, so let us stand together, shoulder to shoulder in the work (v. 30). Our battle is for the gospel of Christ, the salvation of our souls, the glory of Christ, and the welfare of God's elect. Let us devote ourselves whole-heartedly to the cause of Christ.

Be willing to make whatever sacrifice may be necessary for the furtherance of the gospel. Do whatever is within your power to do for the glory of Christ. Do you need any other motive, other than the glory of Christ? Endeavour to earnestly and faithfully serve the welfare of God's elect while you live upon this earth.

Chapter 4

The Life And The Death Of A Believer

For to me to live is Christ, and to die is gain.

(Philippians 1:21)

The Apostle Paul, whose heart's desire was that 'Christ shall be magnified in my body, whether it be by life or by death', made this statement, 'For me to live is Christ, and to die is gain'. Do you see how closely these two words follow each other in our text, 'live', 'die'? There is little more than a comma between them. In reality, there is but a brief distance between life and death! In fact, there is none. Life is the vestibule of death.

Our pilgrimage on earth is but a journey to the grave. The pulse-beat that preserves our life also beats our death march. The blood which circulates life through these bodies is floating us onward to the depths of death. Today we see our friends in health. Tomorrow we hear that they have died. Yesterday we held the hands of a strong man. Today we visit him in the funeral parlour. An hour ago we were riding in the car, fellowshipping with our friend. In a few more hours, we will follow the black hearse that carries him to the home of all living.

Death is closely allied to life. All of us, the youngest and the oldest, the weakest and the strongest, must soon die. Life in this world, at its very longest, is but a very brief thing. 'Our days on the earth are as a shadow, and there is none abiding' (1 Chronicles 29:15). Job said, 'My days are swifter than a weaver's shuttle ... O remember that my life is wind' (Job 7:6, 7). 'We are but of yesterday, and know nothing, because

33

our days upon earth are a shadow' (Job 8:9). 'Now my days are swifter than a post: they flee away … They are passed away as the swift ships: as the eagle that hasteth to the prey' (Job 9:25, 26). 'Man that is born of a woman is of few days, and full of trouble. He cometh forth like a flower, and is cut down: he fleeth also as a shadow, and continueth not' (Job 14:1, 2). 'We all do fade as a leaf' (Isaiah 64:6). 'What is your life? It is even a vapour, that appeareth for a little time, and then vanisheth away' (James 4:14).

As I look in the mirror every morning, I see two things: I see a living man, and I see a dying man. I have lived long enough to know that death is no respecter of persons. I have buried babies, and toddlers, and young children. I have buried old men and young men. I have buried mothers and daughters. I have seen in one family, the father, the son, and the grandson, all taken to the grave in a matter of only a few months.

Will you lay to heart the things that I am saying? Will you lift your heads up from this earth and realize that you are all men and women who must soon die? Here are four facts that are always evident to me. The longer I live, the more weighty these four facts become.

1. I have one life to live
The days that are past are gone and can never be recalled. What is done is done! What have I done for the good of mankind? What have I accomplished for the welfare of God's church? What have I done for the furtherance of the gospel and the glory of Christ? For most of us, those questions are painful. We have spent the years of our lives, our strength, and our labour pursuing vanity!

2. I have one death to die
Death is the fruit of sin … I must die. It does not matter where I die. It does not matter when I die. It does not matter what the cause of my death may be. The only thing that matters is how I die. To die in faith, to die in hope, to die in Christ is a blessed departure from this world. But to die without faith, without hope, without Christ is to enter into eternal misery.

3. I have one judgment to face
Like all of you, after death, I must stand before God in judgment. 'For we must all appear before the judgment seat of Christ; that every one

may receive the things done in his body, according to that he hath done, whether it be good or bad' (2 Corinthians 5:10).

4. I have one eternity to spend
We are living in a world where all things are temporary, vanishing, and passing away. We are going to a world where all things are eternal. The bliss of the righteous is an eternal bliss. The misery of the damned is an eternal misery. And our condition and estate in eternity will be determined by our relationship to the Lord Jesus Christ in this world.

With these things in mind, listen to our text again. Paul was in prison at Rome. Death was staring him in the face. Yet, he gave this testimony, 'For me to live is Christ, and to die is gain.' I wonder how many of us, if any, could honestly make such a testimony. I know this, every true believer lives by faith in Christ, for the glory of Christ; and for all true believers, death is gain.

In our text, 'For me to live is Christ, and to die is gain,' Paul plainly deals with two things: first, the believer's life, and second, the believer's death.

The believer's life
'For to me to live is Christ.' In those words, Paul describes the sum and essence of every true believer's life. He speaks with confidence of his own relationship with Christ. 'For me to live is Christ.' But he is also telling us that which is true of every believer. Those who are born of God live to Christ. We live from Christ. We live by Christ. We live for Christ.

It was not always so. There was a time when we were like all other men; without hope, without God, without life, without Christ in this world! We only began to live in Christ when God the Holy Spirit convinced us of our sin, and of the desperate evil of our hearts, and, when by grace, we were brought to see the dying Saviour making propitiation for our sin.

From that moment, when by faith we saw the slaughtered Lamb of Calvary and cast our souls upon him to be saved, redeemed, and justified, when we saw the virtue of his atonement and the greatness of his grace, we began to live in him. Now, Christ is our Life. Our life is in Christ, and our life is Christ in us (Colossians 1:27; 3:3).

These words are true of every man and every woman who lives by faith in Christ. 'For to me to live is Christ.' It is no longer I that live, but Christ liveth in me (Galatians 2:20). The believer derives his life from Christ (John 10:27, 28). We were lost, but he found us. We were full of sin, but he washed us. We were blind, but he gave us sight. We were naked, but he put the robe of righteousness upon us. We were dead, but Christ gave us life.

The believer's life is sustained by Christ (John 6:56). To live by faith is to live continually upon the blood and righteousness of the Lord Jesus Christ.

The believer's life is fashioned after Christ. I suppose that every living man has a model by which he endeavours to shape his life, a pattern and example which he follows. This is what I am saying, every true believe is a follower of Christ (Revelation 14:4). We do not follow Moses. We do not follow men, nor their customs, traditions, and opinions. We follow Christ.

However, the primary idea conveyed by these words in Philippians 1:21 is that Christ himself is the end and the object of the believer's life. From the day of his conversion to the day of his death, Paul aimed at one thing; he sought one thing; he lived for one thing; he was motivated by one thing: the Lord Jesus Christ (Philippians 3:4-14).

Paul sought the glory of Christ in all things and above all things. He laboured unceasingly for the good of Christ's church and people. He lived and died to preach the gospel of Christ.

What do you live for? Can you, with honesty, say, 'For to me to live is Christ?' I hope you know, by experience, what I am talking about. I recognize that the believer's dedication, devotion, and faithfulness to Christ, at best, is fickle, sinful, and shameful. But I know also that every true believer, from the depths of his heart, wants to live for Christ alone. In his heart of hearts, he has said, 'I have nothing in this world that I have not given to Christ'.

> Here, Lord, I give myself to Thee;
> 'Tis all that I can do.

Are you willing to spend and be spent, to sacrifice and be sacrificed, to give and to be given for Christ? If so, then you can say, 'For me to live is Christ.' Read Luke 14:25-33. If you can truthfully say, 'For me to live is Christ', then you can also say, 'And to die is gain'.

The believer's death

Here is Paul's second point. Every true believer, every child of God, every justified sinner can speak these words with confident assurance: 'And to die is gain'. This is one of those gospel riddles that confound the unbelieving. Only those who know Christ can truly understand this language. John Newton wrote,

> The Lord has promised good to me,
> His Word my hope secures.
> He will my strength and portion be
> As long as life endures.
>
> And when my heart and flesh shall fail,
> And mortal life shall cease,
> I shall possess within the veil
> A life of joy and peace!

Christ is the believer's gain in life. Even here, upon this earth, in Christ we have all, and abound. He is all in all to my soul. Jesus Christ is made to me all I need. All I want, all I can wish for, all that I desire is in Christ. Christ is enough.

Christ is the believer's gain in death. In death Christ is our Hope, our Comfort, our Expectation, our Glory, our All.

Death is not something to be dreaded and feared by God's elect; to die in faith, to die in Christ is gain. Our Lord was revealed to take away the fear of death (Hebrews 2:14, 15). We need not weep for those who die in the Lord; they have received the greatest possible gain. When the believer puts aside this robe of flesh, he will immediately enter into a nobler, richer, more glorious habitation (2 Corinthians 5:1-6). Then, all his prayers and all his best desires shall be granted!

To die, I say, is to gain. It is freedom from sin, the fellowship of Christ, the company of the redeemed, everlasting joy and peace, immortality and eternal glory.

The true believer will lose nothing by his death. For us, to die is gain. No sooner shall we close our eyes in death than we shall enter into the eternal inheritance which was prepared for us by our Father in his eternal decree, purchased for us by our Saviour at Calvary, and for which we have been preserved by the grace of God the Holy Spirit. The fact is, the believer never dies. He just falls asleep in Christ.

If you are wise, you will learn to look upon this world and your life in this world in the light of eternity (2 Corinthians 4:17, 18). Children of God, the day of our opportunity will soon be over. Let us live for Christ!

Chapter 5

The Believer's Rule Of Life

Only let your conversation be as it becometh the gospel of Christ.
(Philippians 1:27)

We believe and preach salvation which comes to sinners as the gift of divine grace alone. We believe and preach that the grace of God in salvation is free, sovereign, irresistible, and effectual. In doing so, I realize we are preaching that which is contrary to the pride of man, the wisdom of man, and the religion of man. The gospel we preach ascribes the whole of salvation to the grace of God, and grants nothing to the free-will, the works, and the merits of men. The gospel of the grace of God, which we cherish, places us in direct opposition to the churches, preachers, and religious leaders of the world around us.

The only redemption we have is the particular, effectual redemption of our Substitute, Jesus Christ (Galatians 3:13).

The only righteousness we have before God is the righteousness of our Substitute (Jeremiah 23:6).

The only acceptance we have with God, in time and in eternity, is the acceptance of our Substitute (Ephesians 1:6).

The only reward we will ever receive from God is the reward of an eternal inheritance, earned for us by the merits of our Substitute, Jesus Christ (Ephesians 1:11).

This is what I am saying: our salvation, our acceptance with God, our preservation, and our reward in heaven does not, in anyway, depend upon our works. There is no point between the gates of hell and the gates of heaven at which God looks upon the works of his elect, either good or bad, to determine what our relationship to him will be, or how he will deal with us.

God looks upon his people in his Son; and seeing us in his Son, he declares that we are perfectly righteous at all times and for all eternity. Being in Christ, united to him by faith, 'We are not under the law, but under grace'. Do you see what this is telling us? We are not justified by the law (Romans 3:20). We are not sanctified by the law (Galatians 3:3). We are not motivated by the law (2 Corinthians 9:7). We are not governed by the law (1 Timothy 1:5-9).

The law of God is not, in any sense, the believer's rule of life, be it the ten commandments given to Moses, or the ceremonial law of the old covenant, or the judicial practices of Israel. 'Christ is the end of the law for righteousness to everyone that believeth.' We have both fulfilled the law's requirements and satisfied the law's penalty in the Person of our Substitute, in the life and death of the Lord Jesus Christ.

When critics hear us preach the gospel of God's grace and hear us affirm the believer's freedom from the law, they accuse us, as they did Paul, of being antinomians. They say things like, 'Such doctrine leads to licentiousness', and 'If what you are saying is true, "Let us sin that grace may abound",' and 'If you believe that, then we can live any way we like, for we have no motive to serve God and no rule of life'. Their speech betrays their hearts. Such gospel-critics as these require the iron bars of the law to restrain them because inwardly they are raging beasts. Nevertheless, their accusations and insinuations are false.

True believer's do have a rule of life. Our rule of life is the gospel of Christ. This is what Paul shows us in Philippians 1:27. 'Only let your conversation be as becometh the gospel of Christ: that whether I come and see you, or else be absent, I may hear of your affairs, that ye stand fast in one spirit, with one mind striving together for the faith of the gospel.'

The gospel of the grace of God in Christ is our rule of life, and it does not lead to licentiousness, but to true godliness. If I am a saved person, the only motive, the only governing principle I need to rule my life is the gospel of Christ.

The word 'conversation' does not merely refer to our talk and speech one to another. It signifies our whole course of life and behaviour in this world. The word literally refers to the actions and privileges of citizenship. We are to have exercise our whole citizenship, all our actions as citizens of the New Jerusalem, as becomes the gospel of Christ. This is what Paul is saying. The law of Christ's kingdom is the gospel; the rule of our citizenship in Zion is the gospel of Christ.

Notice the difference between the exhortations of the legalists and those of the gospel. The legalist will have you to work in order to be saved, or to avoid punishment, or to earn some reward from God. But he who knows the gospel of the grace of God urges you to godliness, because you are saved. The legalist motivates his followers with fear and envy. The gospel preacher motivates the Lord's people with gratitude.

Paul is saying to us, make your actions conformable to your position, live what you are! You profess to be saved by the gospel; you say you glory in the gospel, you say you desire to extend the gospel; then 'let your conversation be as it becometh the gospel of Christ.' He is saying, 'You are citizens of the heavenly Jerusalem; your salvation is absolutely secure in Christ; now act like men and women who are born of God.'

Love for Christ and gratitude for the gospel will motivate, rule, and govern the Lord's true people. Slaves must have the whip of the law to keep them in line, but loving children need only to be reminded of the generous inheritance their Father has given them to stir their devotion to him and motivate their heart. Love is stronger than law. Grace is more powerful than guilt. Gratitude is more persuasive than fear.

What is the gospel?

There is but one gospel. You can catch Paul's definition of the gospel in two words. He calls it the gospel 'of Christ'. The gospel is Christ. If you know Christ, you know the gospel. If you do not know Christ; his Person, his righteousness, his redemption, and his exaltation, you do not know the gospel. Christ is the gospel (Romans 1:1-4).

Christ is the Author of the gospel. In the council chambers of eternity, the Son of God proposed to become the Surety of God's elect. In the fulness of time, he worked out salvation for as many as the Father had given him.

Christ is the Matter of the gospel. It is impossible to preach the gospel without preaching the Person, the work, the offices, and the character of the Lord Jesus Christ. If Christ is preached in the fulness of his redemptive glory, the gospel is preached. If Christ is put in the background, the gospel is not declared. Jesus Christ the Lord is the sum total, the warp and woof, the heart and essence of the gospel (1 Corinthians 2:2). To preach the gospel is to preach: the glory of his person, the purpose of his incarnation, the perfection of his righteousness, the efficacy of his redemption, the meaning of his exaltation and the certainty of his return. Anything less is not the gospel!

The gospel is Christ's property. It is His gospel. It originated with him. It was revealed and declared by him. It glorifies his Person. It proclaims his work. It praises his accomplishments and it is the sweet savour of his name.

Christ is the finisher of the gospel (Isaiah 53:10-12). In the business of salvation Christ is everything. It is all his work and his work alone. He is the author and the finisher. He is the Alpha and the Omega. He is the first and the last. He is the beginning and the end. He laid the foundation stone and he will put the last finishing stroke to the work. Christ does not begin the work then leave it for us to finish. He does it all!

Charles Spurgeon, the eloquent Baptist preacher, said, 'As his hand first tore away the sin which doth so easily beset us, and helped us to run the race with patience, so that same hand shall hold out the olive branch of victory, shall weave it into a chaplet of glory, and put it about our brow.'

Christ is the good news of the gospel (2 Corinthians 5:18-21). The gospel is the 'good spell', the 'good news' or the 'good message' of Jesus Christ. The gospel is emphatically good news! The gospel says, God and man are reconciled, sin is put away, righteousness is established, atonement is made, justice is satisfied, redemption is obtained, and grace is proclaimed.

Living in a manner becoming the gospel

It is my heart's desire to live in this world in such a way that my life shall both glorify the Lord my God and honour the gospel. I want to 'practise what I preach'. That being true, the rule of my life must be the gospel of Christ, which I preach. We do not live by the rules of religious tradition. We do not live by the rule of human opinion. We do not live by the rules of the law. But we do, we must, live by the rule of the gospel.

The gospel is very plain and simple. It is unadorned. It has no ornaments of intellectualism or ritualism. It is 'not with enticing words of man's wisdom'. Yet it is sublime in its simplicity. Let those who believe and preach the gospel be plain and simple people. Our adornment should be the ornament of true grace (1 Peter 3:3, 4).

Believers are transparent men and women, as was Nathaniel who was 'an Israelite indeed, in whom is no guile'. We should be unsophisticated in our attitudes, ambitions, and our lifestyle. 'Except ye be converted, and become as little children ye shall not enter into the kingdom of heaven.'

The gospel of Christ is pre-eminently true. You and I must be truthful, honest men and women, both in our speech and in our business. A believer should never need to take an oath. His word should be as good as an oath. His 'yea' should be 'yea', and his 'nay' should be 'nay'.

The gospel of the Lord Jesus Christ is bold and courageous. There is a foolish sentiment today that people call 'Christian love' but it is an enemy to the gospel. It says, 'Never tell anyone they are wrong. Never say anything about other religions. Never denounce anything as heresy.'

Let people call us 'sectarians'. They may say that we are hard and divisive, but the gospel of Christ demands that we be bold and fearless. Hear what the Word of God says, 'He that believeth and is baptized shall be saved; but he that believeth not shall be damned.' No compromise! No alternative!

The Lord Jesus Christ said, 'All that ever came before me are thieves and robbers: but the sheep did not hear them.' The Apostle Paul said, 'If any man preach any other gospel unto you than that ye have received, let him be accursed.'

I know this is strong language but if we would honour our God this is the way you and I must think and live. I must hold to everything I see taught in the Word of God. I will not even give up little pieces of truth. I must preach the gospel of the grace of God with emphatic clearness, denouncing as heresy everything that opposes it. I must live in the light of God and the sight of God as I believe I should live; and when men say their best or their worst about it, it shall be no more to me than the chirping of a cricket.

The time has come for those who know and believe the gospel to stand faithful, bold, fearless, and defiantly for the gospel. The gospel of Christ gives a man backbone. It gives him firm ground upon which to plant his feet.

The gospel of Christ is gentle. Christ says, 'Come unto me, all ye that labour and are heavy laden, and I will give you rest.' A believing man must be a man, firm, bold, and fearless; but he must be a gentleman, tender, thoughtful, and kind. Someone said, 'He must have a lion's heart and a lady's hand.' There should be such a gentleness about us that little children are not afraid to come to us, and that the publicans and harlots are not driven off by our austerity, but attracted and invited by our mildness.

The gospel of Christ is full of love. He that loves is born of God. Without this grace, whatever we may think of ourselves or what others may think of us, we are really, in God's sight, as sounding brass and tinkling cymbals.

The gospel of Christ is a gospel of mercy. If you would live in such a way as is becoming of the gospel of Christ, you must be a man of mercy, a woman of mercy. Mercy is generous, forgiving, helpful, unselfish, and kind.

The gospel of Christ is righteous and holy. If you would live in a manner that becomes the gospel, you must live by principles of righteousness, truth, and holiness. Do what you know to be right. Avoid that which you know is evil.

The amusements and pleasures of this life, so far as they are innocent, belong to us as they do to other men and women, but when they become evil, or even doubtful, we must discard them. We have joys this world cannot know. We do not need to drink at that muddy river for which worldlings are so thirsty.

Do you want to know how you should live, what you should do, how you should dress, where you should go, and how you should treat your fellow-travellers in this world? Do you want to live in such a way that you honour God, glorify Christ, and adorn the gospel in your life? If you are a believer, I know these things are of real concern to you, for your heart is motivated by love, gratitude, and grace. Let these gospel principles be your rule of life, but do not allow anyone to bring you again under the yoke of the law.

Our rule of life is the gospel of Christ. Obey the gospel and you will honour your Redeemer. Do that which is true and honest. Live boldly and fearlessly for Christ. Be a gentle person. Walk in love. Imitate Christ in mercy. Do what you know to be right.

Why should we live by the rule of the gospel?

There are three things that stand out in Philippians 1:27 as reasons for living by the gospel rule. First, we are motivated by gratitude. Second, we are inspired by love. Third, we are strengthened by faith.

Our lives should be governed by the gospel of Christ because we are citizens of the heavenly Jerusalem and heirs of eternal life. We should be devoted to the glory of Christ our Redeemer. The glory of Christ is the ambition, the desire, the motivating force of every believing heart.

We live by the rule of the gospel for the welfare of Christ's church and for the unity of our brethren. 'That whether I come and see you, or else be absent, I may hear of your affairs, that ye stand fast in one spirit.' Paul is saying, 'If you will so live as men and women in a manner becoming the gospel of Christ, you will be a people of one heart and mind. Nothing can divide you.'

We must live by the rule of the gospel for the furtherance of the gospel. 'With one mind striving together for the faith of the gospel.' We have but one purpose upon this earth. We must make known to all men the gospel of the free-grace of God in Christ. Let us strive together as one body, putting our shoulders to the work.

The pastor must strive together with his people, and the people with their pastor, for the faith of the gospel. The pastor's work is to preach and write and do the work of an evangelist. Your work is to bear constant witness to the truth of the gospel, support the preaching of the gospel, and pray for the success of the gospel.

'Let your conversation be as it becometh the gospel of Christ.' Let us live by the rule of the gospel. Let us live to honour the gospel. And let us live for the furtherance of the gospel.

Chapter 6

The Distinguishing Gifts Of Divine Grace

For unto you it is given in the behalf of Christ, not only to believe on him, but also to suffer for his sake.

(Philippians 1:29)

There are certain truths which the Apostle Paul never allows us to forget. There are certain essential, fundamental truths of the gospel which he teaches in every epistle, and reaffirms again and again in almost every chapter of his inspired letters. There are certain points of gospel truth which characterized Paul's preaching. Everywhere he went, every time he preached, there are certain things he was sure to say. If Paul himself were preaching to you now, I am sure that before he finished his sermon, in one way or another, he would tell you these five things:

1. That which God purposed in eternity he will most certainly accomplish. He would declare the sovereign character of God, and say, the Lord our God is that God whose purpose shall stand. We trust a God whose purpose cannot be frustrated or defeated. All things come to pass and are accomplished, 'Being predestinated according to the purpose of him who worketh all things after the counsel of his own will' (Ephesians 1:11). The Lord Jehovah declares, 'Yea, I have spoken it, I will also bring it to pass; I have purposed it, I will also do it ... My counsel shall stand, and I will do all my pleasure' (Isaiah 46:11, 10).

47

2. The blood of Christ shed at Calvary is an effectual atonement for sin. Paul did not believe the modern atheistic philosophies about the atonement. He proclaimed that the blood of Christ was a real atonement for sin, and in his death the Lord Jesus Christ actually accomplished the redemption of God's elect.

Paul believed in a particular and effectual redemption, and he preached it. He said, 'Christ hath redeemed us from the curse of the law (Galatians 3:13). 'By his own blood he entered in once into the holy place, having obtained eternal redemption for us' (Hebrews 9:12). Paul did not preach the possibility of redemption, or the possibility of atonement. He preached an accomplished redemption, by which all the sins of all believers were, at one time, put away. Christ has actually 'put away sin by the sacrifice of himself' (Hebrews 9:26).

3. Salvation is accomplished by the grace of God alone. Paul would have nothing to do with the free-will fundamentalists, the sacramental papists, or the good works Pentecostals. His preaching rang the clear sounding trumpet of sovereign grace. 'By grace are ye saved through faith; and that not of yourselves: it is the gift of God: not of works, lest any man should boast' (Ephesians 2:8, 9). 'So then it is not of him that willeth, nor of him that runneth, but of God that showeth mercy' (Romans 9:16). With Paul it was grace, grace, grace! When speaking of the matter of salvation, his pen could not spell, and his tongue could not pronounce 'works' or 'merit'. If Paul were preaching here right now, he would tell you in no uncertain terms that salvation was planned by grace, purchased by grace, performed by grace, preserved by grace, and perfected by grace.

4. The Apostle Paul would be certain to also assure God's elect that our heavenly Father is ruling and governing all things in his sovereign, universal providence for the eternal good of his own chosen people. He would look in the faces of the Lord's troubled children, and say to you who carry heavy burdens on your hearts, fear not, 'For we know that all things work together for good to them that love God, to them who are the called according to his purpose' (Romans 8:28). He would say, children of God, rejoice, your Father is on the throne, and he is ruling all things in this world, both good and evil, both pleasant and painful, even down to the most minute details of your life, for the accomplishment of his own eternal purpose, for the glory of his own great name, and for the eternal welfare of his elect. Your heavenly

Father will see to it that all things accomplish eternal good for your souls.

5. If Paul himself were preaching, I am sure he would tell us that all that we are and all that we experience as believers must be attributed to the distinguishing grace of God. He would be sure to ask you, 'Who maketh thee to differ from another? and what hast thou that thou didst not receive? Now if thou didst receive it, why dost thou glory, as if thou hadst not received it?' (1 Corinthians 4:7). In Philippians 1:29, Paul is doing just that. He is again reminding us of the distinguishing grace of God. He shows us two distinguishing gifts of divine grace. 'For unto you it is given, in the behalf of Christ', first, 'not only to believe on him, but', second, 'also to suffer for his sake'.

In these words, Paul tells us that both our faith in Christ and that which we suffer for Christ's sake are gifts of divine grace, privileges granted and bestowed upon God's elect. Try to get a mental picture of Paul's purpose in this passage. The children of God at Philippi were suffering many things from many adversaries because of their faith and obedience to the gospel. Paul, who was also suffering for Christ as a prisoner in Rome, wanted to do two things. He wanted to tell them – and us – what God expects of his children, and he wanted to encourage them – and us – to fulfil that expectation.

What does God expect of his children? (vv. 27, 28). Our attitude toward Christ and his gospel must be one of tenacity. We must stand fast in the Lord, rooted and grounded in him, trusting him and clinging tenaciously to the faith and truths revealed in the gospel. Where the gospel of the grace of God in Christ is concerned, we must not give an inch.

Our attitude toward one another must be one of harmony. In one spirit, with one soul, we must strive together, shoulder to shoulder, as one man, for the faith of the gospel. There must be no discord among us. We who believe the gospel must be in full agreement in our purpose and work for the furtherance of the gospel and the glory of Christ. We have such a noble cause that we cannot afford to allow trivial matters to divide us.

Our attitude toward the enemies of the gospel must be one of fearlessness. Our Lord's enemies, those who are the enemies of the cross of Christ, must be counted as our enemies (Psalm 139:20-22). We must face them, confront them, and oppose them fearlessly, 'In nothing terrified by your adversaries'. There is no room for compromise or cowardice. To compromise the gospel, for any reason, is cowardice, and cowardice is to betray our Lord.

This is what God expects of his children: tenacity in adhering to the gospel, harmony in the work of the gospel, and fearlessness in the face of our enemies.

How can I encourage the people of God to be so thoroughly committed to Christ in the midst of their many trials? I will remind them of the great blessings conferred upon them by the gospel, and the distinguishing privileges they have in Christ. It is as though Paul had said, I will show my brethren that the things which they suffer because of their faith in Christ are tokens of their eternal salvation. 'For unto you it is given in the behalf of Christ, not only to believe on him, but also to suffer for his sake.'

Children of God, I want to encourage you to tenaciously adhere to the gospel, to harmoniously labour together for the furtherance of the gospel, and to fearlessly oppose the enemies of the gospel, by reminding you of these two distinguishing gifts of divine grace, which the Lord our God has bestowed upon us.

1. The privilege of believing on Christ
'For unto you it is given in the behalf of Christ to believe on him.' The faith in Christ which Paul speaks of is not merely believing that he is the Christ, that he lived in righteousness, died as a substitute, and ascended to heaven. Even Satan himself has that kind of faith. This is a mere persuasion of the mind. It is not conversion of the heart.

To believe on Christ, in the Biblical sense of that term, is to surrender your heart to him and to rest your soul upon him. It is to surrender to his dominion and trust his merits. To believe on Christ is to depend upon his accomplished work as your Mediator, Redeemer, and Substitute. To believe on Christ is to trust him, and him alone, for your entire salvation, and then to keep on trusting him.

What is true saving faith? According to the Word of God, there are at least four things essential to what we call 'saving faith'.

Knowledge is essential to faith. Before anyone can truly believe on Christ, they must know him. You cannot worship an unknown God, and you cannot trust an unknown Saviour. In order to truly believe on Christ you must know who he is, why he came into this world, what he has done, where he is now, and what he is doing there. In John 9:35-38, our Lord asked the man who had been born blind, 'Dost thou believe on the Son of God?' and the man said, 'Who is he Lord, that I might believe on him?'

There must be an assent, or an agreement, of the heart with God's testimony concerning his Son. John Owen said, 'Of all the poison which at this day is diffused in the minds of men, corrupting them from the mystery of the gospel, there is no part that is more pernicious than this one perverse imagination, that to believe on Christ is nothing at all but to believe the doctrine of the gospel.' True faith rests not upon the testimony of men, but upon the testimony of God himself in the Scriptures. 'It is written in the prophets, And they shall be all taught of God. Every man therefore that hath heard, and hath learned of the Father, cometh unto me' (John 6:45).

True faith in Christ is the trust, confidence, and dependence of the heart upon him for salvation and eternal life. Faith is a resignation of myself to Christ. Faith is committing my soul into the hands of Christ. Faith is trusting Christ with all, relying upon him for all, and resting in him as my all-sufficient Saviour.

Where there is true faith in Christ, there is love and affection for him. Faith works by love. Love always accompanies true faith. 'If any man love not the Lord Jesus Christ, let him be Anathema Maranatha' (1 Corinthians 16:22). Those who trust Christ love him as he is revealed in the Scriptures. They love him, his Word, his work, and his people.

Where does this faith come from? True saving faith is a gift from God, promised to God's elect in the covenant of grace, purchased for us by the blood of Christ, and performed in our hearts by the gracious operation of the Holy Spirit in regeneration (John 1:12, 13; Ephesians 2:8, 9; Colossians 2:12).

No one has faith, or the ability to exercise faith by nature. No one has the power to create or bestow faith in his own heart, or in the heart of another. Faith in Christ is the gift of God. It is a privilege bestowed upon God's elect by the irresistible grace of God the Holy Spirit. This is God's distinguishing grace.

If you and I believe, it is because God gave us the will and the power to believe. Faith in Christ is a gift of God's goodness and grace. Grace bestows it. Grace causes it to grow. Grace motivates it. Grace causes it to act. Grace preserves it.

This faith has been given to us 'in the behalf of Christ'. God gives faith to his elect for Christ's sake, upon the merits of Christ's righteousness and shed blood, and for the glory of Christ.

How does the Spirit of God create faith in dead sinners? God the Holy Spirit creates faith sovereignly, by his irresistible power in regeneration. But the Word of God makes it plain that he always uses the instrumentality of gospel preaching to produce saving faith in the heart.

Here are four impossibilities (Romans 10:14-17). No one can call upon Christ in true faith until they believe on Christ in their heart. No one can savingly believe on Christ until they hear the gospel of Christ. No one can hear the gospel of Christ without a preacher. No one can truly preach the gospel of Christ in the power of the Holy Spirit unless he is sent of God.

Children of God, here is one excellent motive to inspire you to that tenacity, harmony, and fearlessness of which we have spoken and with which God expects his children serve. Pause and think on this: God has distinguished you from the rest of mankind by bestowing upon you the great privilege of believing on Christ! 'For unto you it is given in the behalf of Christ, to believe on him.'

2. The privilege of suffering for Christ

You may say, 'Pastor, did you say, the privilege of suffering?' No, I said, 'The privilege of suffering for Christ'. Suffering is not a privilege in itself. Everybody in this world has to suffer, both those who are lost and those who are saved. But there are few in this world who have the privilege of suffering for Christ.

Only of God's elect can it be said, 'For unto you it is given in the behalf of Christ, not only to believe on him, but also to suffer for his sake.' Only to the elect has this privilege been granted.

You may be sure of this: if you tenaciously cling to the gospel, if you harmoniously labour for the furtherance of the gospel, if you fearlessly defend the gospel, if you are truly committed to the gospel of Christ, you will suffer; but your suffering will be a very light thing to you, for you are privileged to suffer for Christ (Acts 5:41).

John Gill said, 'The same persons to whom is given to believe in Christ, to them it is given to suffer for him: and they all do in some shape, or another.'

We do not suffer for Christ in the same way that he suffered for us. His sufferings were vicarious, as the Representative and Substitute of his people; our sufferings are personal. His sufferings were infinite; our sufferings are temporal and slight. His sufferings were undeserved; our sufferings are much less than we truly deserve. His sufferings were punitive to satisfy justice, our sufferings are corrective as tokens of love. His sufferings were for our sins; our sufferings are for his glory. His sufferings were meritorious; our sufferings merit nothing. Nevertheless, God's elect do suffer in the behalf of Christ, for his sake.

What does it mean to suffer for Christ's sake? In one sense, a very great sense, to suffer for Christ's sake is to suffer our pain, affliction, and adversity in patient faith, submitting to it as the will of God, trusting the wisdom and grace of divine providence in it, and seeking to glorify Christ by it.

But in this passage, Paul is talking about that which the believer voluntarily, wilfully endures, because of his faithfulness to Christ and his gospel (Matthew 10:22-24, 34-40; Luke 14:27, 33).

To suffer for Christ's sake is to give up or sacrifice anything for the gospel. It is to endure any hardship or adversity for the gospel. It is to willingly, knowingly make trouble for yourself for the gospel's sake (1 Peter 2:20-24). To suffer for Christ's sake is to take up your cross and follow him.

Why is it a privilege for God's elect to suffer anything for Christ's sake? To suffer for Christ's sake brings the believer into nearer communion and fellowship with his Redeemer (Hebrews 13:13). To willingly suffer anything for Christ's sake is an assuring token of Divine favour (John 15:19-21; 1 Peter 4:14). A believer who suffers for Christ's sake will be a means of winning unbelievers to Christ, and encouraging the devotion and commitment of other believers (Philippians 1:12-14). All that we might suffer for Christ's sake will be more than rewarded in eternity (Romans 8:18; 2 Corinthians 4:17; 2 Timothy 2:12; 1 Peter 4:13).

I say to you, my brothers and sisters in Christ, tenaciously cling to the truths of the gospel. Harmoniously labour for the furtherance of the gospel. Fearlessly oppose the enemies of the gospel.

Let us do these things, by the grace of God, for the glory of God. 'For unto you it is given in the behalf of Christ, not only to believe on him, but also to suffer for his sake.' Let us therefore believe him. And let us willingly suffer whatever need be for his sake.

Chapter 7

Imitating The Incarnation

'If there be therefore any consolation in Christ, if any comfort of love, if any fellowship of the Spirit, if any bowels and mercies, fulfil ye my joy, that ye be likeminded, having the same love, being of one accord, of one mind. Let nothing be done through strife or vainglory; but in lowliness of mind let each esteem other better than themselves. Look not every man on his own things, but every man also on the things of others. Let this mind be in you, which was also in Christ Jesus: Who, being in the form of God, thought it not robbery to be equal with God: But made himself of no reputation, and took upon him the form of a servant, and was made in the likeness of men: And being found in fashion as a man, he humbled himself, and became obedient unto death, even the death of the cross. Wherefore God also hath highly exalted him, and given him a name which is above every name: That at the name of Jesus every knee should bow, of things in heaven, and things in earth, and things under the earth; And that every tongue should confess that Jesus Christ is Lord, to the glory of God the Father.'

(Philippians 2:1-11)

In this passage of Scripture, the Apostle Paul is admonishing us to live in our daily conduct in a manner that is becoming the gospel of Christ. He is encouraging us to unity of Spirit, mutual love and affection, humility, and lowliness of mind, and real care and concern for one another. He is telling us how a believer should live in this world, and why. He not only shows us how we ought to live as believers, but he gives us a supreme example to follow. The whole basis of his appeal is that which the Lord Jesus Christ has done for us.

Consolation in Christ
This world is a place of pain, sorrow, trouble, and grief. Job said, 'Man is born unto trouble, as the sparks fly upward (Job 5:7). 'Man that is born of a woman is of few days, and full of trouble' (Job 14:1). The sons of Adam, as they have known life, have known trouble. Because man has defiled the world with sin, the world brings sorrow upon man. Sin is man's nature, and sorrow is his reward. Even those who are redeemed by Christ and born again by almighty grace are not exempted from pain, sorrow, trouble, and grief in this life. Jeremiah, God's faithful servant, is known to us as 'the weeping prophet'. He said, 'I am the man that hath seen affliction … He hath filled me with bitterness, he hath made me drunken with wormwood' (Lamentations 3:1, 15). Our Lord told us very plainly, 'In the world ye shall have tribulation' (John 16:33).

You read your Bible day after day, searching for consolation. You call upon the Lord in prayer, seeking consolation. You go listen to God's servant preach, hoping for some word from God that might give you consolation. Where can a troubled soul find consolation? The Apostle Paul tells us, 'If there be therefore any consolation in Christ.' The word 'consolation' means 'comfort' or 'confidence'. Consolation is the most soothing, most desirable, most precious thing in all the world to the heart full of trouble and sorrow.

Where can I find consolation? Is there any consolation in Christ? Paul asked the question rhetorically. Of course there is, and you who know him have experienced it often. The fact is, true consolation, such as can reach the heart, is found nowhere except in Christ. He is here saying, if you have experienced consolation in Christ, show that experience by loving your brethren. If you have found sweet encouragement in the gospel of Christ, show that sweetness and encouragement to your brethren. If you expect consolation in Christ, console your brethren in Christ. Never once does Paul take us back to the law as a basis or rule to motivate us. His whole argument is drawn from the gospel. He presses us to our duty of love in a most tender and loving manner. He says, 'If there be therefore any consolation in Christ'. Consolation is one of heaven's most precious gifts. Like all the gifts of heaven, it is in Christ. The Lord Jesus Christ provides strong and everlasting consolation for those whom he has bought with his own precious blood.

The Holy Spirit, during the gospel age, is revealed to us as the Comforter. It is the Holy Spirit's business to cheer and console the hearts of God's people. It is true, he does convince us of sin. He does illuminate and instruct us. But the primary work for which he has been sent into the world is to lift up those who are pressed down, make glad the hearts of his renewed ones, and to bring consolation to God's elect.

The Holy Spirit is the Comforter of the church. This age is peculiarly the age of the Holy Spirit, in which Christ cheers our hearts not by his personal presence, as he shall do in eternal glory, but by the indwelling presence of the Holy Spirit in our hearts as the Comforter. The Holy Spirit is the Comforter, but Christ is the Comfort. The Holy Spirit consoles, but Christ is the Consolation. If I might use a metaphor, the Holy Spirit is the Physician, but Christ is the Medicine.

The Spirit of God comforts the people of God by taking the things of Christ and applying them to our hearts. The Holy Spirit heals our wounded spirits and aching hearts by applying the blood and grace and power of Christ to us. He cheers our souls by showing us the things of Christ. Here is a blessed promise to cheer our souls, 'I will not leave you comfortless: I will come to you' (John 14:18).

Our Lord's history is a long and eventful one, but every step of it yields comfort to the children of God. If we trace his steps from the highest throne of glory to the cross of deepest woe, and then follow him through the grave and up again to the shining majesty of heaven, throughout every part of that wondrous pathway, we will surely find the flowers of consolation growing in abundance.

Love's incentive
Next, Paul says, 'If any comfort of love'. If we enjoy the comfort and strength of God's love, the everlasting love of the Father, the redeeming love of the Son, the quickening love of the Spirit, and the brotherly love of grace, that love which is so pleasant and delightful, then we should give to one another the comfort and strength of mutual love. If we have any genuine grounds of hope in Christ, founded upon his Person, his righteousness, his death and his intercession, then we ought to comfort one another.

Have you found any comfort in God's love for you in Christ? If you have found comfort in Christ's love, then abound in that love toward others. Share that comfort with your brethren. Have you been comforted by the love of your brethren for you? Then show love to your brethren.

'If any fellowship of the Spirit.' If we have been brought into fellowship with God and one another by the spirit of grace, then we should strive to maintain and build upon that fellowship.

'If any bowels and mercies.' If we have any real depth of affection, if we have any real compassion and concern for Christ, his glory, and one another, if our religion is real, if it is more than lip service to God, let us show to each other love and concern. If these things are not in us, if they do not flow from our hearts to the hearts and lives of our brethren, then our religion, our profession of faith, our doctrinal orthodoxy, and moral uprightness is nothing but a vain show of hypocrisy!

Here is the incentive for Christian love. The love which we have experienced from Christ, from our brethren, and from God's servants should be displayed by us to others.

Love directed

Paul gives us three general directives to follow. He is saying, if you would show the love of Christ to one another, here are three things which must characterize your attitude and actions toward one another. If you would live in a manner becoming the gospel of Christ and adorn the doctrine of God our Saviour, follow these three principles of conduct.

The first thing that should characterize God's people is unity. Like those early disciples, every church family should be known by their unity, their oneness of heart, of mind, and of purpose. Let us have the same love. Let us love the same things, have our minds set on the same objects, and see to it that our hearts pull together in the same direction. If these things are in you, Paul says, 'Fulfil ye my joy, that ye be likeminded, having the same love, being of one accord, of one mind' (v. 2). Nothing brings greater joy to God's servants than the sight of God's people displaying love, affection, and concern for one another. Let the heirs of heaven, the children of God, believers in Christ, and the family of God be likeminded; one in love, affection, and care, one in unity, harmony, and peace, one in mind, purpose, and desire! These things reveal the reality of our faith. These are the marks, fruit, and evidences of inward grace.

Paul is saying brethren should be known for their love to one another. Believers are the family of God. A family, if it is what it ought to be, is bound together and made strong by cords of family love. Paul reminds us that as we have been the objects of love, we should be the dispensers of love.

Second, lowliness of mind and disposition should characterize the people of God. 'Let nothing be done through strife and vain glory' (v. 3). Nothing should be done through strife, or passion, or contention. Nothing should be done in pride. There is no greater enemy to the unity of the church, the gospel of Christ, and brotherly love than pride and self-importance among the Lord's professed people. Anything that is done through strife dishonours God. Anything that divides brethren is a reproach to Christ. Anything that is born of contention casts a slur upon the gospel of the grace of God. The source of strife, division, and conflict between brethren is always vain-glory, pride, self-seeking, self-serving pride. Love is not selfish, but self-denying and self-sacrificing. Believers live not for themselves, but for the glory of God, the gospel of God, and the people of God.

'In lowliness of mind let each esteem other better than themselves' (v. 3). We should quickly observe the defects and infirmities of our own, but readily overlook and make allowances for the defects which our brethren may have. We must esteem each of our brethren in Christ more highly than we esteem ourselves. We know ourselves best, and we know our own worthlessness and corruption. Any man who knows himself will not find it hard to esteem others highly and himself lowly.

Third, Christian love should characterize the people of God. Here Paul is talking about the fellowship and unity of the church. 'Look not every man on his own things, but every man also on the things of others' (v. 4). He is saying, look not every man upon his own interests, but upon the interests and welfare of his brethren. Do no ask, 'Is this the best thing for me?' Rather ask, 'Is this the best thing for my brethren?' He is saying the way to promote unity, peace, fellowship, and love is not to look out for yourself, but look out for one another. Do not seek your praise; seek somebody else's praise. Do not promote yourself; promote someone else. Do not be concerned about your own feelings; be concerned about your brother's feelings. We must be severe on our own faults but charitable on those of others. Christian love is helpful, it really seeks the welfare of God's people.

Love's motivation

Why should we be willing to abase ourselves? Why should we set aside our own desires, ambitions, and preferences for the sake of others? Upon what grounds can anyone make such an appeal? Do you need a motive for such a manner of life as Paul has described? Look to your Saviour, your Redeemer, your Lord.

'Let this mind be in you', this loving, self-abasing, self-sacrificing mind, 'which was also in Christ Jesus' (v. 5). In order to redeem us, the Son of God lived and died in lowliness and humility. Words cannot express the depths of his humiliation. He came 'not to be ministered unto, but to minister and give his life a ransom for many'. Our Lord thought not of himself, but of us. He served not himself, but us. In his life, he left us an example to follow. He says, 'Do as I have done'. This must be our rule of life. 'Let this mind be in you, which was also in Christ Jesus.'

Who is the Lord Jesus Christ? 'Who, being in the form of God, thought it not robbery to be equal with God' (v. 6). Paul assures us that Jesus Christ is God. He is declaring that the Man Christ Jesus is the very nature and essence of God, the express image of his Person. The Man, who is our Redeemer, is our God. Because he is God, our Lord Jesus justly claimed equality with God in all things. The Man Christ Jesus is himself God almighty, God the eternal Son.

What has the Lord Jesus Christ done? He 'made himself of no reputation, and took upon him the form of a servant, and was made in the likeness of men' (v. 7). The Son of God emptied himself of all the brilliance of his glorious Person which had forever shone forth from him in the courts of heaven as the Son of God. He robed himself in human flesh, concealing his glory as God from all eyes except the eyes of faith. He was not forced into servitude, but he willingly 'took upon him the form of a servant', by his own voluntary act. He was, in reality, in his inmost soul, a servant in voluntary subjection to the Father. Throughout the days of his life upon the earth our Saviour lived in total subjection to God as his Servant.

Paul tells us that God's own Son 'was made in the likeness of men'. Our Lord Jesus was holy, harmless, undefiled, and separate from sinners. His human nature was incapable of sin. Yet, it was a real human nature. Like us, he ate when he was hungry, slept when he was weary, wept when he was in sorrow, and cried out to God when he was in agony of soul. He knew all the weaknesses, pains, temptations, and fears of humanity. The only thing about humanity he never knew was sinning.

Jesus Christ, our Saviour, really is one of us. The Son of God, assumed human nature, lived in righteousness as the Representative of his people, suffered and died at Calvary as the sinner's Substitute, satisfied the law and justice of God for all who believe, rose from the dead, and ascended to the throne of God. Our heart leaps within us when we think of the coming of Immanuel! God with us, in our nature, brings the dawning of hope to sinners. 'Thanks be unto God for his unspeakable gift.'

'And being found in fashion as a man, he humbled himself, and became obedient unto death, even the death of the cross' (v. 8). We owed obedience to the law which we could not render. But Christ rendered that obedience and paid that debt for us. Our Lord Jesus rendered obedience not only to the law of God and the Word of God, but to the entire will of God. It is Christ's obedience to God as our Representative which constitutes our righteousness, justification, and redemption. Our Saviour went to the cursed tree with joy and delight in his soul, to suffer the wrath of God for us, to do his Father's will.

What is the result of our Lord's humiliation? 'Wherefore God also hath highly exalted him, and given him a name which is above every name; That at the name of Jesus every knee should bow, of things in heaven, and things in earth, and things under the earth; and that every tongue should confess that Jesus Christ is Lord, to the glory of God the Father' (vv. 9-11). Because of his humiliation, his obedience, his sufferings, and his death as our Substitute, the Lord Jesus Christ has been exalted to the throne of universal dominion (Isaiah 53:10-12; John 17:2).

Love's example
By means of Christ's incarnation, peace and pardon are accomplished. Now, God can be just and the justifier of all who believe. Here, in the incarnate God-Man, every attribute of God is revealed in perfect

harmony; the law of God is magnified, the grace of God in the gospel is revealed, the sinner is saved, and God is glorified.

We should meditate upon our Lord's incarnation and imitate the example of love, humility, and compassion he has given us in his incarnation. As we imitate him, we will both honour our God and do good to our brethren.

May God give us grace that we might follow our Lord's example, ever submitting to and delighting in obedience to our Father's will. 'Let this mind be in you, which was also in Christ Jesus.'

Chapter 8

'He Humbled Himself'

And being in fashion as a man, he humbled himself, and became obedient unto death, even the death of the cross.

(Philippians 2:8)

It is my prayer that the Lord will enable us to enter into the meaning of these words, 'he humbled himself'. Someone once asked me the question, 'If Jesus was Mary's Son, how could he also be her God?' To the human mind, that appears to be a most reasonable question. Scoffers and sceptics have ridiculed the gospel of Christ for two thousand years, because human reason can find no suitable answer to that question. It is a snare by which Satan has taken many to hell. Many heretical and damnable religious cults have been established with the basic idea that it is not reasonable to believe that Jesus Christ is both Mary's son and Mary's God.

The fact is, this question, 'If Jesus was Mary's son, how could he also be her God?' cannot be answered upon terms of human wisdom. Volumes of books have been written by well-learned and well-meaning men, in an attempt to answer this one question. But to human wisdom, it still remains a mystery. But our faith is not built upon human wisdom. Faith takes God at his Word. Faith believes the record God has given concerning his Son. Faith does not always understand God, either his Word or his ways. How can it be true that Jesus Christ is both Mary's son and Mary's Lord? For the believing heart, three words answer the question sufficiently: 'He humbled himself.' Faith needs no further explanation, nor does she desire more.

Christ is God, the eternal Son, who in the fulness of time, Paul tells us, 'being in the form of God, thought it not robbery to be equal with God; But made himself of no reputation, and took upon him the form of a servant, and was made in the likeness of men: And being found in fashion as a man, he humbled himself, and became obedient unto death, even the death of the cross' (Philippians 2:6-8).

The Lord Jesus Christ is 'God manifest in the flesh'. He is 'over all, God blessed forever'. He is our God, the sovereign, eternal Creator, glorious, and majestic. In order to redeem us and save us, he has taken upon himself our nature. He is the God-man.

We worship the Triune God, as he is revealed in Holy Scripture, Father, Son, and Holy Spirit (1 John 5:7).We worship Jesus Christ the Lord as God (John 1:1-3, 14; Hebrews 1:1-3). We rejoice to know this God humbled himself to assume our nature, in order to redeem us from our sins (Galatians 4:4, 5). He who is our Saviour is, and must be, both God and man. He is as truly God as though he were not a man, and as truly man as though he were not God.

Paul's purpose in this chapter of Philippians is to unite the people of God in bands of holy love. In order to do so he takes us immediately to the cross. Paul knew that in order to create unity, you must first promote humility. Men do not quarrel with one another when their ambitions have come to an end. When each is willing to be the least, when everyone desires to place his brother higher than himself, there is an end to strife, schism, and division. Now, in order to create this lowliness of mind, under the teaching of the Holy Spirit, Paul spoke about the humiliation of Christ. He would have us to humble ourselves, so he tells us how that our Lord and Master humbled himself. In order to redeem us, save us, and reconcile us to God, the Lord Jesus Christ 'humbled himself'.

What Christ has done
'Being found in fashion as a man, he humbled himself, and became obedient unto death, even the death of the cross.' As we look as this verse, we will take the words just as they stand. Here the Apostle Paul lays before our hearts the facts of our Lord's humiliation. He shows us four steps of that ladder by which the Lord of glory descended into the

depths of his infinite humiliation. We cannot begin to measure the extent of our Saviour's humiliation. But if God the Holy Spirit will just allow our hearts to realize it our limitations and enter into it nevertheless by faith, our souls shall be greatly profited by it. Let us remove our shoes from off our feet for we are about to tread on 'holy ground'.

First, 'Being found in fashion as a man'. Behold, the Son of God is now the Son of Man! If we stopped here, and said no more, this is humiliation enough to astonish the angels (Genesis 3:15; Isaiah 7:14).

Our Lord assumed not the nature of angels, but the nature of fallen man (Hebrews 2:17). His human nature was incapable of sin, and did no sin. Yet, it was a real human nature. He is a real man. He veiled his Godhood in this world as a child. He lived in poverty. He laboured as a carpenter. For thirty-three years, he lived in silent humility as a man. As a man, he was tempted of Satan. As a man, he suffered weakness, hunger, and thirst. As a man, he had many inward struggles that drove him to prayer (Hebrews 5:7).

'Who hath believed our report? and to whom is the arm of the LORD revealed? For he shall grow up before him as a tender plant, and as a root out of a dry ground: he hath no form nor comeliness; and when we shall see him, there is no beauty that we should desire him' (Isaiah 53:1, 2). Yet, this is only the beginning of our great Redeemer's humiliation. Our text says, 'Being found in fashion as a man, he humbled himself.' That is to say, after assuming our nature, the Lord Jesus Christ continued to humble himself, as a man.

Second, as a man in this world, our Lord 'became obedient'. Here is the rule of our Lord's humiliation, obedience. In all things, our Saviour was voluntarily submissive to the will of his Father (Psalm 40:7, 8; Isaiah 50:5-7; John 10:17, 18).

As a man, the Lord Jesus Christ learned obedience (Hebrews 5:8). He learned obedience through the Scriptures, by the direction of the Holy Spirit, and through prayer. That which he knew to be his Father's will, he carried out with precise determination. This is true humility. It is a willing submission and obedience to God.

Third, Paul goes yet further and tells us that as a man, the Lord of glory became 'obedient unto death'. The Lord Jesus Christ laid down his life particularly for his own elect and accomplished our eternal redemption by his obedience unto death as our Substitute. Wonder of wonders, God the eternal Son willingly lays down his life in obedience to his Father's will. Surely, there could be no greater depth of humiliation than this! But there is …

Fourth, as a man, the Son of God, 'became obedient unto death, even the death of the cross'. Here is the deep, infinite abyss of humiliation to which our great God voluntarily descended, so that he might redeem his people. This was the great object of the incarnation. Jesus Christ was born at Bethlehem that he might die at Jerusalem as the sinner's Substitute. It is not enough that he assume our nature, live in righteousness, endure temptations and trials, and perfectly obey God's law as our Representative. If he would save us, the Son of God must be 'obedient unto death, even the death of the cross'. Death alone is not sufficient. Immanuel must die the death of the cross!

What does this mean, 'the death of the cross'? It was a violent death. It was an extremely painful death. It was an ignominious, shameful death. It was a penal death, reserved for slaves and the basest of criminals. It was a specifically cursed death. It was the death portrayed by the brazen serpent, and prophesied in the Old Testament Scriptures, 'And they shall look upon me whom they have pierced' (Zechariah 12:10). And the death of our Lord Jesus Christ was a substitutionary death for all who were chosen in him before the world began. 'For Christ also hath once suffered for sins, the just for the unjust, that he might bring us to God' (1 Peter 3:18).

Why Christ humbled himself
Our Lord Jesus Christ humbled himself to establish righteousness in the earth. He humbled himself that he might put away sin. And he humbled himself to justify the guilty. The Lord Jesus Christ actually accomplished the redemption of all his elect and secured their eternal salvation when he died upon the cursed tree. What he intended to do, he has fully done! Christ has redeemed us from the curse of the law and put away the sins of his people. 'Being justified freely by his grace through the redemption that is in Christ Jesus: whom God hath set forth to be a propitiation through faith in his blood, to declare his righteousness for the remission of sins that are past, through the forbearance of God; To declare, I say, at this time his righteousness: that he might be just, and the justifier of him which believeth in Jesus' (Romans 3:24-26). Our dear Saviour voluntarily took on himself our sins and died in our place, because of his great love for us!

The effects of Christ's humiliation

What effects should the humiliation of Christ have upon us? It should give us a great firmness of faith in our Lord's sin-atoning sacrifice. It should create within our hearts a holy hatred of sin. It should teach us obedience. It should inspire us to self-denial and self-sacrifice for him. 'For ye know the grace of our Lord Jesus Christ, that, though he was rich, yet for your sakes he became poor, that ye through his poverty might be rich' (2 Corinthians 8:9).

Our Saviour's humiliation should cause us to hold all human honour and praise in contempt. It should inspire our hearts with an ever-increasing love for the Lord Jesus Christ. Our Lord's humiliation ought to inflame our souls with a desire to honour him.

Chapter 9

The Exaltation Of Our Lord Jesus Christ

Wherefore God also hath highly exalted him, and given him a name
which is above every name: That at the name of Jesus every knee should
bow, of things in heaven, and things in earth, and things under the earth;
And that every tongue should confess that Jesus Christ is Lord, to the
glory of God the Father.

(Philippians 2:9-11)

I want to set before you a picture of our Lord Jesus Christ in his
exaltation and glory. I want us to lift our spiritual eyes up to heaven,
and look within the veil. I do not suggest that you should meditate on
those streets of gold, the walls of jasper, or the gates of pearl. I do not
even suggest that you turn your eyes to that white-robed throng of the
redeemed, who forever sing the loud hallelujahs of the heavenly temple.
I want us to turn our eyes and our hearts to him who sits upon heaven's
exalted throne. It is my prayer that God will enable each of us to see
Immanuel, God in our nature, in the glory, splendour, majesty, and
supremacy of his exaltation. The hymnwriters Watts and Kelly wrote,

> There, like a man, the Saviour sits;
> The God, how bright He shines;
> And scatters infinite delight
> On all believing minds.

The head that once was crowned with thorns
Is crowned with glory now;
A royal diadem adorns
That mighty Victor's brow.

No more the bloody crown,
The cross and nails no more:
For hell itself shakes at His frown,
And all the heavens adore.

Do you see him? Can you begin, in your heart's imagination, to get a picture of him? Behold his transcendent glory! He is King of kings and Lord of lords. He is the Sovereign Monarch of heaven and earth. His empire is as limitless as the universe. His dominion is from everlasting to everlasting. His kingdom ruleth over all! Everything belongs to him. Everything is governed by him. Everything does his bidding. He is God over all and blessed forever.

Standing before his throne are all those angelic, heavenly creatures, who anxiously worship and serve him. They cast their crowns before him in adoring reverence. In that same great assembly, I see all of God's elect who have already entered the heavenly city. Their crowns, too, they cast before his feet, and sing the songs of redeeming love.

I see beneath his blessed feet the earth, which has become his footstool. His saints upon the earth worship, adore, and honour him as the rightful Sovereign of the universe and the rightful Lord of their hearts. I see before this great King all the elements of the world, all the beasts of the field, all of those fallen sons of Adam who wage their warfare against his throne, all the spirits of the damned in hell, the demons of hell, and the prince of darkness himself.

My heart begins to fear for the safety of the great King's throne, his kingdom, his glory, and my own soul. But my fears are silenced. All those men, and demons, and Satan himself have a bit of iron in their mouths and a bridle of steel; and he who holds the reins of that bridle is the King himself! Even as they rage and wage their warfare against him, they are but fulfilling the King's will and purpose. They, too, shall bring glory to the great King.

Children of God, all is well, for Jesus Christ the Lord is the undisputed King of glory. He rules in the blessed serenity of total, absolute sovereignty. If you can but get a believing view of Christ on the throne, in his exaltation and glory, it will bring peace, comfort, and courage to your heart.

The message of Christ's exaltation as Lord is essential to the preaching of the gospel. The gospel of the grace of God is not preached when the Lordship of Christ is denied. This was the constant message of the Apostles. They went everywhere affirming that Jesus is Lord (Acts 2:32-38; 4:10-12; 5:30-32; Romans 14:9). The exaltation of Christ and his universal Lordship is the basis of our hope and of his saving power (John 17:1, 2). To deny that Christ is Lord is to deny the accomplishment of redemption, the sure hope of those who believe, and the security of God's elect (Isaiah 53:10-12).

The heart acknowledgement of Christ's Lordship is essential to saving faith (Romans 10:9, 10). No one is truly saved and converted until he acknowledges and confesses that Christ is his rightful Lord. Faith involves a heart allegiance and obedience to Christ as Lord. Where there is no submission in the heart to Christ as Lord, there is no faith in the heart toward Christ as Saviour (Luke 14:26, 27, 33). Jesus Christ is not your Saviour unless he is also your Lord and King.

As we look at this passage in Philippians 2:9-11, and meditate together on the exaltation of our Lord Jesus Christ, I want to call your attention to four things:

The reason
First, Paul sets before us the reason for Christ's exaltation, 'Wherefore' (v. 9). The exaltation of our Lord Jesus Christ is the reward of his obedience to his Father (Hebrews 10:5-14).

Because our Lord humbled himself and became obedient unto death, even the death of the cross, God the Father has exalted him to the place of supreme honour and majesty (Psalm 2:6-8; Hebrews 1:1-13).

It is not possible for you and I to begin to understand and enter into the meaning of those words, 'He humbled himself', No one can understand the humiliation of Christ except the Triune God. But it is profitable for us to meditate upon it. As I see it, the Scriptures reveal five distinct acts of humiliation on the part of our blessed Redeemer.

His voluntary submission to the Father's will in the Covenant of Grace (Isaiah 50:5-7). His incarnation (2 Corinthians 8:9). His perfect life of obedience to his Father (Hebrews 5:8, 9). His temptation as a man in the wilderness and in the garden (Hebrews 4:15). His crucifixion and death (Galatians 3:13). Consider the shame of the crucifixion, the physical agony of death by crucifixion, the imputation of sin to him, and his being forsaken of his Father.

All of this, his entire humiliation, he willingly endured as our Substitute, for our salvation.

The exaltation of Christ is the exact reversal of his humiliation. He who was condemned by the law, because of the sin imputed to him, has now been declared righteous by the law, because he has put away sin and satisfied the justice of the law. He who was poor has been made rich. He who was rejected has been accepted. He who learned obedience by the things which he suffered has all power, authority, and dominion given unto him.

As the Scriptures declare our Lord's humiliation, they also set before us the five steps of his glorious exaltation.

His resurrection (Romans 1:4). His ascension (Luke 24:50-52). His coronation (Acts 2:32-36), the Lord Jesus Christ, God's Son, David's Son and his Lord, has taken his rightful place upon the throne of David. His universal reign (Psalm 110:1-4). The consummation of all things for the glory of his name (Revelation 5:13).

The reality

Second, I want you to know the reality of Christ's exaltation. 'Wherefore God also hath highly exalted him, and given him a name which is above every name.' The exaltation of our Lord Jesus Christ is not some bit of fanciful speculation. It is not that he shall be King. He is King! It is not that he shall have sovereign and universal dominion. Right now, Jesus Christ our Saviour is the reigning Monarch of the universe!

The Lord Jesus Christ did not exalt himself to be King, but God the Father exalted him. Men did not exalt Christ, but God exalted him. There is a lesson for us here. Let us not exalt ourselves, but wait for our heavenly Father to exalt us (James 4:10). Though we may be despised and dishonoured by men, we care nothing for it. If we are obedient to our God, in his time, he will exalt us to his throne. 'He that humbleth himself shall be exalted' (Luke 14:11).

The exaltation which Paul speaks of is the exaltation of our Saviour's humanity. As God the Son, our Saviour needed no exaltation. He is equal with the Father in all things. The symbols of his glory were laid aside for a while. He wrapped his Godhead in mortal flesh. Now his human nature, in union with his eternal Godhead, has been exalted to the throne of glory. It is the God-man who stooped to shame, sorrow, degradation, and death, who now sits upon the throne of heaven.

In the exaltation, our Lord Jesus Christ resumed the glory which he held with the Father from all eternity; and in his glorious humanity, he assumed the very glory of God!

The realm

In the third place, I want us to take notice of the realm of Christ's exaltation. God the Father has 'given him a name which is above every name: that at the name of Jesus every knee should bow, of things in heaven, and things in earth, and things under the earth'.

In those words, Paul is telling us that all the vast empire of God's creation has been placed under the dominion of the Son of God, our Saviour. He is telling us that there is no limit to the realm and sphere of our Redeemer's total sovereignty. He is Lord of all! He is Lord of all people and Lord of all things. The name which God has given him is 'Lord Supreme'.

Jesus Christ is Lord over all people upon this earth, both the righteous and the wicked, both the living and the dead (Romans 14:9).

Jesus Christ is Lord over all the powers of darkness. Those souls damned forever in hell, the demons of hell, and Satan himself are under the dominion of the Lord Jesus Christ. Not one of our great King's enemies can breathe or move, except by his permission; and then their moves are governed by Christ to accomplish his own eternal purposes.

Jesus Christ is Lord over all the vast regions and inhabitants of heaven. He who is heaven's King is our Saviour, Mediator, Substitute, and Advocate. The King of the City Beautiful is Immanuel.

Jesus Christ is Lord over all the affairs of providence (Hebrews 1:1-3; Romans 8:28). Children of God, I rejoice to tell you that there is no place in the universe, from the throne of eternal glory to the lowest pit of the deepest hell, where Jesus Christ does not rule in total, sovereign, absolute power. God's creation is not out of control. Nothing is thrown into confusion. Jesus Christ is Lord!

The results
Fourth, I want us to observe the results of Christ's exaltation. 'Wherefore God also hath highly exalted him, and given him a name which is above every name: That – in order to accomplish this purpose – at the name of Jesus every knee should bow, of things in heaven, and things in earth, and things under the earth; and that every tongue should confess that Jesus Christ is Lord, to the glory of God the Father.'

Here are five blessed facts that shall most certainly come to pass as a result of the exaltation and glory of the Lord Jesus Christ.

1. Mercy is extended to a fallen race. Because God has put this universe into the hands of a Mediator, mercy has been extended. Had it not been for God's purpose to provide a suitable Mediator to save his people, this world would have been destroyed as soon as Adam fell. A door of hope is opened for fallen man because there is a Man in glory!

2. The pleasure of God, his entire purpose, shall be accomplished (Isaiah 53:10). The whole purpose of God has been placed in the hands of his Son, our Mediator. The purpose of God is safe because his Son now reigns upon an immutable throne (Isaiah 45:22-25).

3. All of God's elect shall be saved (John 17:2). Because Jesus Christ reigns as Lord, he shall see of the travail of his soul and shall be satisfied. He died to redeem us, and he lives to save us. 'He shall not fail'.

4. Every intelligent creature in the universe shall acknowledge and confess that Jesus Christ is Lord, and rightfully so. The angels of heaven and the demons of hell, the vast multitude of the redeemed in glory, and the numberless spirits of the damned, and Satan himself shall all bow before the throne of the Lamb and confess, 'Jesus Christ is Lord. It is right that he should be Lord. We acknowledge his rightful dominion over us. All his works are works of righteousness, justice, and truth. Christ is Lord!' When the great King comes in his glory, every knee shall bow to him, and every tongue shall confess, 'Jesus Christ is Lord'. My soul anxiously anticipates that day! And,

5. God the Father shall be glorified in all his vast creation through his Son (Romans 11:33-36). In that day all things shall be reconciled to God. That is to say, the Lord God shall display his matchless glory in

all that he has done and in all that he has allowed to be done throughout the ages of creation's existence. We shall see all things in their true light. We shall nod our heads and say, 'Yes, Amen. That is right. God has done what was best. Now, I see how that he is glorified in all things.' Read Revelation 19:1-6. All events shall be reconciled to him, for the glory of his name. All the damned shall be reconciled to the glory of his justice. All the redeemed shall be reconciled to the glory of his holy name in all things.

I beg you to consider one more thing. How do we recognize and acknowledge the exaltation and glory of our Lord Jesus Christ? We submit to him as Lord. We trust him in all things. We are content with his good providence. We commit ourselves and all that we have to the honour and glory of his name. May the Lord our Redeemer graciously hasten that day when his glory shall be revealed.

Chapter 10

'Work Out Your Own Salvation'

Wherefore, my beloved, as ye have always obeyed, not as in my presence only, but now much more in my absence, work out your own salvation with fear and trembling. For it is God which worketh in you both to will and to do of his good pleasure ... Yea, and if I be offered upon the sacrifice and service of your faith, I joy, and rejoice with you all. For the same cause also do ye joy, and rejoice with me.

(Philippians 2:12-18)

Paul gives us a very practical admonition. It is a most reasonable exhortation. And it is easy enough for us to understand. That admonition is, 'Work out your own salvation'. Let it be understood that this admonition is not addressed to men and women who are unbelievers. It is not addressed to those who are unsaved, but to those who are already saved. It is not addressed to those who are lost, but to those who are evidently the children of God, to those who already possess eternal life, to those who are already the heirs of eternal glory.

One very basic principle to follow in interpreting Scripture is that you must determine to whom a given passage is addressed. It is not possible to determine the meaning of any text until you know who the text is speaking to, believers or unbelievers. In this passage, Paul is speaking to men and women who are already believers. His admonition to us as believers is that we must 'work out our own salvation'.

These things we know. They are evidently taught throughout the Word of God.

No one is saved by works (Romans 3:20; Galatians 2:16)
Salvation is not to be attributed to man in any measure whatsoever. God demands perfection. He will not accept any substitute for perfection. The holiness, righteousness, and justice of God's character will not allow him to accept sincerity, or the best works that you can do. He demands perfection! He will not accept anything less than perfection. He will not bless anything less than perfection. He will not reward anything less than perfection, and no man is capable of rendering perfect obedience to God.

If it were possible for a man to be saved by his own works, then the gospel of Christ that we preach would be foolishness indeed. If salvation could be obtained by works, then Christ died in vain. If salvation could be gained by works, then the glory of it must be attributed to man. Pride and boasting would be encouraged. If man could be saved by his own works, he would have no incentive to worship, love, and obey God.

Salvation by works is a blasphemous, criminal doctrine. It robs God of the glory of his grace and robs Christ of the glory of his redemption, because it makes both grace and redemption needless things.

Salvation is by grace of God alone (Ephesians 2:8, 9; Romans 9:16)
God saves sinners by grace through faith. Salvation and eternal life are graciously bestowed upon sinners through the merits of Christ's righteousness and shed blood. Our only hope of acceptance before God is in the Substitute, Jesus Christ. All the blessings of God's grace are freely bestowed upon sinners through the merits of Christ, without any works of their own.

Election, redemption, regeneration, justification, sanctification, preservation, and glorification are works of grace. And even the faith, by which we receive Christ and all the blessings of grace in him, is a work of grace in our hearts. Augustus Toplady wrote:

> Not to myself I owe,
> That I, O Lord, am Thine;
> Free-grace hath all the shades broke through,
> And caused the light to shine.

Me Thou hast willing made
Thy mercy to receive;
Called by the voice that wakes the dead,
I come to Thee and live.

Why was I made to see,
Although by nature blind?
Why am I taken home to thee,
And others, left behind?

Because Thy sovereign love
Was bent the worst to save;
Jesus who reigns enthroned above,
The free salvation gave.

No more a child of wrath,
Thy smiling face I see,
And praise thee for the work of faith,
That thou hast wrought in me.

Our salvation is an accomplished reality. We contributed nothing to it. Our salvation was accomplished in the purpose of grace before the world was. Our salvation was accomplished in the purchase of grace at Calvary. Our salvation was accomplished in the power of grace in regeneration.

Though we have not yet entered into the full enjoyment of eternal glory, it is as surely ours as if we were already among the glorified saints in heaven. If any of us obtain salvation, it will be by grace alone, trusting the merits of Christ the sinner's Substitute.

This salvation, which is accomplished by the grace of God alone through faith in Christ, will produce good works (Ephesians 2:10; Titus 2:14; James 2:14-20).

Those who accuse us of promoting licentiousness and antinomianism by preaching the gospel of God's pure, free-grace, accuse us falsely. Any man who professes faith in Christ whose heart and life are not altered and brought into conformity with the grace of God is a liar. His profession is false. He is a lost man.

I do not say that God's people are without sin, or that there are certain acts of gross evil which the people of God will not commit. But I am saying that in the general tenor of their lives, the people of God live consistently with those 'things that accompany salvation'.

Paul's admonition in this text is that we must work outwardly, in our lives, that salvation which God has wrought in our hearts by his mighty grace. 'Work out' means to outwardly work the inward grace, or to work out of the inward principle of grace in the heart. It does not mean 'complete the work which God has begun'.

'Wherefore, my beloved', writes Paul. As you read this admonition within the immediate context, you will see that the basis of Paul's appeal to us is threefold.

Since Christ has given you the example of unrestricted, voluntary obedience to the Father, 'Work out your own salvation'.

Since God exalts those who humble themselves and honours those who honour him, 'Work out your own salvation'.

Since the God-man, our Mediator in heaven, imparts strength to those who trust him and yearn to obey him, 'Work out your own salvation'.

Then, in Philippians 2:12-18, Paul answers four questions for us.

1. What are we to do? (v. 12)

For the most part, the believers at Philippi had always been obedient to Christ and his gospel. But there was a danger which Paul spotted. These people had a tendency to lean too heavily upon Paul. When he was present with them they tried very hard to please him and win his approval. Paul is saying to them, your obedience and service must be to God, not to me. It is as though Paul were saying, 'I am no longer with you to help you and guide you, as a father helps his toddling children. You must now work out your own salvation without me to guide you. Each of you must live before God on your own.'

It seems clear to me that Paul's admonition to us includes at least three things:

First, as believers in this world, we must actively engage ourselves in those things which accompany salvation. Paul's exhortation could be translated, 'Work about your salvation'. Employ yourself in those things which are consistent with salvation. Paul is saying, do not become dormant and passive. But actively serve the Lord your God. Be busy in public and private worship, in submission to the gospel, in seeking grace to know and obey God's will in all things. Paul is saying, go on your course in cheerful, loyal, active obedience to Christ to the end of your days.

Second, as the children of God, we must serve the Lord in our generation. One of the very old translations makes Paul's exhortation read like this, 'Do the work, or business of your lives'. Do the work which God has for you to do in your generation. Do with all might what God has prescribed for you by providence, directed you to do by his Spirit, taught you to do by his grace, and constrains you to do by his love.

This is the day which the Lord has given us. I want to serve him in it. When I am gone, and my work is ended, I hope I shall have contributed something to the spiritual good of my generation for the glory of God. This is my life's task.

Third, we who are saved by the grace of God must live as men and women who are saved by the grace of God (Titus 2:10). That which is the inward principle of our hearts will be evident by the general conduct of our lives. Those principles are gospel graces of honesty, compassion, forgiveness, patience, and faith.

It is one thing to shout, 'Do all to the glory of God', it is another thing to practise it. It is one thing to say, 'We forgive those who trespass against us', but something altogether different to forgive when we have been wronged. It is one thing to hang up a beautiful plaque in your hallway that reads, 'Christ is the Head of this Home', it is something else to submit all things in your home to him. It is one thing to say, 'I believe in the sovereignty of God', and it is another thing to trust the God who is sovereign in all our circumstances.

This is what I am saying, brethren, 'Work out your own salvation'. Let every man and woman who is saved by the grace of God live according to his or her profession.

Perhaps you say, I want to honour the Lord in my life. I want to live for the glory of Christ, but …

2. Where do we find the strength for our work? (v. 13)
Paul answers that question for us in this verse. He says, Children of God, you can do it. You can work out your own salvation, 'For it is God which worketh in you both to will and to do of his good pleasure'.

God gives his people the will to serve him by implanting a new nature in our hearts in regeneration. In the new birth the Lord gives us a new heart and a new nature that is willing to submit all things to the glory of Christ. That man who is born again by the grace of God desires above all things the glory of Christ. In his heart he is committed to, consecrated to, and dedicated to, the glory of Christ (Romans 7:18).

God gives his people the strength to do what he would have them to do by his indwelling Spirit. The Spirit of God dwelling in us is the Divine energizer of our lives, enabling us by grace to do the good that we do. The good that we do is mixed with much evil. The good we do is not to be attributed to us, but to God the Holy Spirit who dwells within us (John 15:4).

Both the will and the strength to do anything for the glory of God is given to us according to his good pleasure. What is done by us for the glory of God is pleasing to him. Though our 'good works', if we may call them such, are full of sin and unworthy of God's acceptance, they are pleasing to our heavenly Father. Our works are acceptable to God through the merits of Christ. The Lord looks upon the motive of our hearts, which he has created within us, and says, 'In as much as my child truly desires to honour me, I am honoured by him' (Psalm 147:11; 149:4).

3. How should God's elect work out their own salvation? (v. 14)

It is not enough that we render a mere outward obedience to the Lord. A mere external compliance with what we know to be right, or with what we know is required of us, will never be accepted by God. 'The Lord looketh on the heart.' God is not so much concerned with our outward actions as he is with our inward attitude. There are some things that we can, we should, and we must do; but they must be done in the right spirit and with the right attitude, or God is not honoured by them.

All true obedience is heart obedience. Paul tells us that each of us must 'work out our own salvation with fear and trembling ... doing all things without murmurings and disputings'. We must serve the Lord in 'fear', in reverence and awe. We must serve the Lord with 'trembling', in faith and humility. And we must serve the Lord without murmuring against him, as though that which he requires of us is grievous.

God does not want, and he will not accept anything given or done in his name grudgingly (2 Corinthians 9:7; 1 John 5:1-3). Those who serve

God outwardly, but inwardly rebel against the very service they perform, performing it only from a sense of duty, do not know the grace of God.

We must serve the Lord without disputings, or without argument and hesitation. John Gill said that which is 'the will of God should be done at once, without dispute upon it, or hesitation about it, however disagreeable it may be to carnal sense and reason. The will of God is not to be disputed, nor flesh and blood consulted in opposition to it.' 'To him that knoweth to do good, and doeth it not, to him it is sin' (James 4:17).

4. Why must we apply ourselves diligently to this work? (vv. 15-18)
In these verses, Paul inspires us to live a life becoming the gospel we profess. He has told us to 'work out our own salvation'. He has told us where we find strength for such a life and he has told us how we are to perform our life's work. Now he is going to motivate us, stir us up, and give us a reason to do what we all know we ought to do.

He gives us three powerful, persuasive arguments for a life of submission, service, obedience, and dedication to the Lord Jesus Christ, our God and Saviour.

First, he tells us to do those things which are consistent with our salvation for the glory of God. We are God's representatives in this world. We are the children of God in the midst of a crooked and perverse generation. As such, we should be blameless and harmless before men. We ought never to give any man grounds for justifiable, legitimate complaint against us. Our Father's name is at stake!

Second, Paul exhorts each of us to live in a manner that is becoming the gospel of God, for the gospel's sake. We are to shine as lights in this world, 'Holding forth the word of life'. All that the men and women among whom you live and work know about the gospel of Christ is what you tell them about it, and what they see of it in your lives.

Third, each of us are exhorted to live to the glory of God for the joy of God's church as a whole. When the whole church family strives together day by day to honour Christ, the whole family rejoices. When even one member of the family is disgruntled, rebellious, contrary, and unbecoming of the gospel, the whole family suffers.

'Work out your own salvation.' May God the Holy Spirit effectually apply these words to our hearts and enable us to live in this world as men and women who have the grace of God in their hearts. If men and women are saved by the gospel I preach, I will most gladly pour out my life as a sacrifice to the Lord in his service. If the gospel that I preach causes you to live for the glory of Christ, my labours will not be in vain.

Chapter 11

Three Faithful Servants Of God

Yea, and if I be offered upon the sacrifice and service of your faith, I joy, and rejoice with you all. For the same cause also do ye joy, and rejoice with me. But I trust in the Lord Jesus to send Timotheus shortly unto you, that I also may be of good comfort, when I know your state ... Him therefore I hope to send presently, so soon as I shall see how it will go with me. But I trust in the Lord that I myself shall come shortly. Yet, I supposed it necessary to send to you Epaphroditus, my brother, and companion in labour, and fellowsoldier, but your messenger, and he that ministered to my wants ... Because for the work of Christ he was nigh unto death, not regarding his life, to supply your lack of service toward me.

(Philippians 2:17-30)

This passage speaks of three faithful servants of God: Paul, Timothy, and Epaphroditus. These three men are examples of what every preacher should be. Before we look at these three men, but using them as examples, I want to give you some characteristics of every faithful minister.

There is in our day an almost universal contempt for preachers. Far too often, even in those places where God has blessed a congregation with a faithful pastor, there is a disdain for the preacher and the work of the ministry. This ought not to be. We dare not make too little of the office and position which God's servant holds. He is God's servant.

The highest office in the world is to be a preacher of the gospel. I want to do what I can to magnify my office in my generation. The most demanding work in all the world is to be a faithful pastor. And a faithful pastor should receive the highest honour and respect in all the world.

The preacher is just a man, but he is God's man. If he is truly God's servant, he is God's voice, God's spokesman, God's representative to his people. He should be treated and received as such.

The Apostle Paul tells us plainly what the qualifications are for those who are set apart for the work of the gospel ministry (1 Timothy 3:1-7; Titus 1:5-9). A pastor must be a man who believes and preaches the gospel of Christ. No man has any business in the pulpit who does not believe and preach the gospel of God's free, sovereign, and effectual grace in Christ.

A pastor must be a man who is gifted for the work of the ministry. There are many who desire to preach the gospel who are not gifted to preach the gospel. There are many who go into the ministry, for one reason or another, who have no gifts for the work. But you may be sure of this, if a man is called of God to preach the gospel, he will be gifted by God for the work of preaching the gospel. He must have a clear understanding of gospel truth. He must be able to communicate divine truth in simple language and clear terms.

A pastor must be a man who has proven his commitment to the glory of Christ, his concern for the people of God, and his faithfulness to the gospel (Acts 15:26). A novice should never be given the responsibility of the gospel ministry (1 Timothy 3:6). We do not need 'preacher boys' in our pulpits. We must have men of experience, men who have proven themselves to be fit for the work.

If a man in the congregation is not known to be a man of faithfulness, dependability, and reliability, he has no business in the ministry. Someone might say, 'But where does a man get the experience that will prove his faithfulness?' He will prove himself in his church life, in his home life, and doing his job.

A pastor must be a man who is reputable and influential. Paul said, he must be a man of 'good report of them which are without' (1 Timothy 3:7). He must be a man who rules his own house well, a man who is sober minded. He must be a man who is generous and given to hospitality. He must be a man who is not selfish and greedy.

What is the work of the gospel ministry?
I want you to know something of the work and burden of the gospel ministry. In order for you to pray for your pastor, support him, and assist him in the work of the gospel, you need to understand what that work involves.

The Word of God clearly defines the work of God's servants. God's servants, all of God's servants, are preachers! First and foremost, a pastor must be a preacher. If a man gives himself wholeheartedly to the work of preaching the gospel, he will have time for very little else (1 Timothy 4:12-16; 2 Timothy 2:15; 4:1-5).

The work of the gospel ministry, the whole work of the gospel ministry, is preaching the gospel of Christ. That work demands all of my time, all of my care, and all of my attention. God's servant must give himself relentlessly to the public proclamation of the gospel, at home and abroad, as God opens the door.

Every faithful pastor is a diligent student of Holy Scripture, and he must be a man of prayer. A pastor must use his pen as well as his mouth in the proclamation of the gospel. Often that which is written has a far wider audience and a far more lasting impact upon men than that which is spoken.

What is the responsibility of God's people to God's preachers?
The greatest blessing which God can give to any church, or congregation of believers, is a man who faithfully preaches the gospel of Christ. The greatest curse which God can bring upon any people is for him to silence the voice of his servant.

You are to receive God's servant as God's messenger to you (v. 29). You are to honour those who preach the gospel for their work's sake (1 Thessalonians 5:12, 13). You are to submit yourselves to those whom God places over you (Hebrews 13:7, 17), and obey the word of God which they preach to you. A pastor must lead the people of God by example as well as by speech, and you are to follow the example of faith they set before you.

Working together, a pastor who is faithful to the gospel of Christ and people who are faithful to God's servant can accomplish much for the glory of Christ.

Now, let us consider those three faithful servants of God in our text, as I point out certain characteristics which they exemplify.

Paul, the self-sacrificing apostle (vv. 17-19, 23, 24)
In all things, Paul proved himself faithful. He was an example to all believers in this world and to all who preach the gospel. Paul was a rare man indeed. There were many things which set him apart from other men. But, as I read the life and letters of this great man, I see four things which stand out as characteristics I desire to imitate.

First, Paul was a man of unbending faith. He believed God. He trusted Christ and followed Christ. Never once after his conversion do we see Paul acting in a manner contrary to faith in Christ. He lived by faith in Christ. He walked by faith in Christ. He died by faith in Christ (2 Timothy 1:12). Paul was every inch a man; and he was a man of faith.

Second, Paul was a man of self-sacrificing, self-denying devotion to the gospel of Christ (Acts 20:24). Paul lived to preach the gospel. The gospel of Christ was his meat and drink. Everything he was and everything he had was devoted to the gospel.

Any family relation or any friendship he had which might hinder his service to Christ was immediately broken off and disregarded.

His life was a perpetual sacrifice to the gospel of Christ. It seems almost natural that such a man as this should die for preaching the gospel. He was faithful unto death (2 Timothy 4:6-8).

Third, Paul was a man of unquestioning submission to the will of God. He went where he went, did what he did, said what he said, and suffered what he suffered in quiet, patient submission to the will of God. He committed himself to the will of God (Philippians 4:11).

Fourth, Paul was a man of unrelenting love for the people of God. As our Lord loved the church and gave himself for it, Paul loved the church and gave himself to it. Even while he was in prison at Rome, awaiting the executioner, his concern was for the welfare of God's elect (v. 19).

Timothy, the faithful preacher (vv. 20-22)
Timothy and Paul had a very close relationship with one another. They were very dear friends. But more importantly, they were companions in the work of the gospel.

Timothy had demonstrated a genuine interest in and love for the people of God (v. 20). Unlike many, even in his day, Timothy was not seeking personal gain by the ministry. He did not seek a name for himself, a place for himself, or earthly riches for himself. His heart's concern was for the welfare of God's elect.

It is a sad fact that in every age the church of Christ has been plagued with men who preach for profit (v. 21), compare, for example, Ezekiel 34:1-6. Timothy had proven his faithfulness to the gospel and the sincerity of his motives by his loyal service with Paul (v. 22).

There are few men like Timothy. He sought nothing for himself. He was like Elisha with Elijah, content to serve God's prophet. He was a preacher, called and gifted of God but he did not thrust himself into the work. He waited for God's time and God's place.

He faithfully served the Lord in the place where God put him. It was best for the gospel's sake, for the people of God, and for the glory of Christ for Timothy to serve in the background for many years; and he did it with patience.

In God's time, the care of the churches was placed upon Timothy's shoulders. When the time came for Timothy to assume greater responsibilities, he was ready. His faithfulness in less noticeable matters had prepared him for faithfulness in greater concerns.

Epaphroditus, the loving pastor (vv. 25-30)
Here Paul is commending Epaphroditus as the loving pastor he was. He was inspiring the Philippians to love their pastor, because he was worthy of their love. He was inspiring them to receive him and honour him, because he was worthy of their honour.

Epaphroditus was God's messenger to his people at Philippi (v. 25). Epaphroditus genuinely loved the people to whom he ministered (v. 26). His care was not for himself, but for the Lord's people.

Epaphroditus faithfully gave himself to the work of the gospel, even when his own health was in danger (v. 30).

Paul had his place, Timothy had his place, and Epaphroditus had his place. Paul was more famous than Timothy. Epaphroditus was not so well-known as either Timothy or Paul. Yet, there was no jealousy between them. They were not in competition with one another. They were brethren, companions, fellow laborers in the gospel. Each one was faithful in the place where God had put him.

Let each of us be faithful in the place where the Lord has put us. We cannot place too much importance upon the value of God's servants to his church. Faithful gospel preachers are to be received by us and treated with honour and respect due their office. Let us faithfully labour together in our generation for the glory of Christ, for the furtherance of the gospel, and for the increase of his kingdom.

Chapter 12

Religion – False And True

Finally, my brethren, rejoice in the Lord. To write the same things to you, to me indeed is not grievous, but for you it is safe. Beware of dogs, beware of evil workers, beware of the concision.

(Philippians 3.1, 2)

The church at Philippi was truly a wonderful congregation. These saints had been dear to Paul's heart for many years. He was the first man to preach the gospel of Christ to them. He was their spiritual father. He had watched this congregation grow from a few young believers, who met in a clearing by the riverside, to a large, flourishing congregation. By the sustaining grace of God, they had remained faithful to Christ and his gospel. They were a source of great joy to God's servant.

The Philippians were doctrinally sound. They were also a very generous and charitable people. They were united in the faith of the gospel. They were zealous missionaries, anxiously seeking the furtherance of the gospel and the conversion of sinners.

When Paul heard that the church at Philippi was being harassed by false teachers, who denied the all-sufficiency of Christ's righteousness and shed blood, he was deeply disturbed. It seemed that a real danger was threatening this beloved church. There were some who had crept into the church who were 'the enemies of the cross of Christ'. They pretended to be God's servants, but they were really the ministers of Satan. They claimed to be preachers of grace, but they were really preachers of works. They came in the name of Christ, but they really

91

opposed Christ. These Judaizers, or legalists, had come in the name of the Lord seeking to impose upon God's saints the law of Moses. They were wolves in sheep's clothing. They did not openly deny Christ and the gospel of the grace of God. But they sought to mix law and grace.

Because of this danger, Paul used vigorous and unmistakable language to warn God's church about these false prophets and the false religion which they were peddling. He knew the jeopardy the church was in. He knew any mixture of law and grace is total denial of grace (Romans 11:6). He knew any doctrine that teaches men salvation can be attained, maintained, or improved by works of personal righteousness is total apostasy (Galatians 5:1-4).

I realize that the greatest danger to the souls of eternity bound sinners is the danger of false religion. The Word of God warns of this repeatedly. Untold multitudes have perished and are perishing today because false prophets have given them a false hope and deceived them with a false religion. Religion without Christ is the most deadly evil in the world. 'There is a way that seemeth right unto a man, but the end thereof are the ways of death' (Proverbs 16:25). 'To the law and to the testimony: if they speak not according to this word, it is because there is no light in them' (Isaiah 8:20). Read: Jeremiah 5:30, 31; 6:13, 14; Ezekiel 34:1-6; Amos 8:11; Matthew 7:13-15; 2 Corinthians 11:1-4, 13-15; 2 Timothy 4:3, 4; 2 Peter 2:1-3; 1 John 4:1.

An exhortation

Let us remember this Epistle was written under the direct inspiration of God the Holy Spirit. It was written not for the Philippians only, but for us also. What Paul says to them he says to us. These things were written for our learning and admonition.

This chapter begins with Paul's final admonition to his beloved brethren at Philippi. He had some strong, stern warnings to give. But his final word to his friends begins with a tender exhortation. He says, 'Finally, my brethren, rejoice in the Lord' (v. 1). He is addressing God's true children, continually admonishing those who truly belong to Christ to rejoice in him.

Life is filled with disappointments, frustrations, and sorrows. But no matter what our circumstances, as children of God, if we have Christ, if we are washed in his blood and robed in his righteousness, we always have reason to rejoice. The more we rejoice in Christ, the more willing we will be to do or suffer anything for his name's sake, and the less likely it will be that anything will draw us away from him. God give us grace to believe Nehemiah's words to the people, 'The joy of the Lord is your strength' (Nehemiah 8:10).

Paul had warned the people of Philippi before of false brethren; now he is about to warn them again, with good reason. 'To write the same things to you, to me indeed is not grievous, but for you it is safe' (v. 1). This is what Paul is saying, 'It is no irksome task to me to warn you of those who would ruin your souls, because I know that you need this safeguard.' Then, in the spirit of faithfulness to Christ and love for the souls of men, Paul denounces all false religion in no uncertain terms, and describes the characteristics of true religion in the simplest terms possible.

A warning
'Beware of dogs, beware of evil workers, beware of the concision' (v 2). The apostle is here giving us a serious warning. He is not talking about men and women from some far eastern cult. He is not talking about those false religions of ancient history; Hinduism, Judaism, or Islam. He is not talking about the idolatrous false religions that have sprung up in more recent history; the Campbellites, Pentecostals, Mormons, or Russellites. Paul is talking about people who claim to be true Christians, men who claim to preach Christ and worship God.

These men and women were members of a church very much like our own, but they had a false religion. Paul says to the true people of God, 'Beware! Beware! Beware!' He uses that word 'Beware' like the blows of a gavel, saying, 'Give me your attention. The danger of false religion is threatening you!' Here he is warning them to take heed and beware of false prophets (Matthew 7:15).

He is talking about every preacher of free-will, works religion. He is talking about every preacher who would attempt to bring us under the yoke of bondage to the law. He is talking about every preacher who makes salvation to be, in any way or to any degree, the work of man. Paul is talking about every false prophet in the world, every man who comes in the name of God, but does not preach the gospel of God's free and sovereign grace in Christ.

Very few people today have ever heard the gospel of the grace of God. Today's gospel emphasizes what the sinner does for God, rather than what God does for the sinner. Mark this well, salvation is something God does for you, not something you do for God. Today's gospel emphasizes heaven and hell, rather than the real issues of Christ and sin. Today's gospel is a message to the head, rather than a message to the heart. Today's gospel calls on men to stand up and be counted, whereas the gospel of God calls on men to bow down and worship.

Paul denounced those who preached a false gospel in the strongest terms possible. He said, 'Beware of dogs.' He calls them dogs because that is what the Word of God calls male prostitutes (Deuteronomy 23:18; Isaiah 56:10, 11). They are those men who prostitute the gospel of Christ and the glory of God for gain. As a dog returns to its own vomit, these men return to legal works. Like mad dogs, they bite and devour God's saints. Being greedy, covetous, self-serving dogs, they make merchandise of the souls of men, and though they claim to be building up the kingdom of God, they are not even in it.

Then, he says, 'Beware of evil workers', referring to those same dogs (preachers) who appear sincere and zealous, but draw attention away from Christ and what he has done, to man and what man is to do. They teach, preach, and promote man centred, works based, free will religion (Matthew 7:22, 23). The good works of religion without Christ are the most abominably evil works done in this world. All works of religion, morality, and righteousness performed by men with the hope of meriting God's favour or turning away his anger are evil works!

Next, Paul warns, 'Beware of the concision'. They called themselves 'the circumcision; Paul calls them 'the concision', flesh cutters. They called themselves preservers of truth; Paul called them perverters of truth. They called themselves healers of strife; Paul called them promoters of strife and division. Those who are of the concision are men and women who teach, in hope of winning God's favour, one should cut, mutilate, and otherwise punish the body. They are men who mutilate the gospel of Christ and the souls of men, not by an avowed denial of the gospel, but by a deceitful corruption of the gospel. Paul is urging us to beware any preacher or any doctrine that elevates man, and what man does. In other words, beware of Christless religion.

False religion
We are plagued in our day with men who have prostituted the gospel of Christ. They are prophets of deceit. The religion they peddle is a false

religion and those who follow them will awake in the day of judgment to find their preachers have led them headlong to destruction. I warn you, for Christ's sake, beware of dogs! Beware of evil workers! Beware of the concision! I lay nine solemn charges against the preachers of our day. I speak plainly and candidly, because the souls of men, the gospel of Christ, and the glory of God are at stake.

1. They preach in the name of God, but rob him of his essential glory as God; His absolute sovereignty, his perfect holiness, and his inflexible justice.

2. They talk much about the sins of men, but say nothing about the sin of man.

3. They preach much about the death of Christ, but deny the efficacy of his blood and the merits of his atonement.

4. They preach much about the love of God, but reduce his love to nothing but a sentimental, helpless passion.

5. They preach 'salvation by grace alone', but the grace they preach is entirely dependent upon the sinner for its power.

6. They preach righteousness, but the righteousness they preach is the righteousness men perform, not the righteousness of God imputed to men in Christ.

7. They preach salvation as an act of the mind and body, rather than a renewal of the heart by sovereign grace.

8. They preach Christ as a Saviour to keep men out of hell, but deny the necessity of surrender to Christ as Lord.

9. They preach those things which men want to hear, and conceal or deny those things which are offensive to men as a whole.

Modern religion reduces the triune God to nothing but a weak, defeated, frustrated figment of man's imagination. Modern fundamentalism worships an idol moulded from the corruption of the human heart, garnished with the ornaments of depraved brains, and painted with the words of false preachers.

Modern religion makes God a spectator, helplessly watching to see what men will do with his creation. It makes Christ a frustrated, defeated failure who has done his best to save men, but his best was not good enough. It makes the Holy Spirit a helpless influence for good which man may either obey or refuse.

True religion

True religion is an effectual operation of divine grace in the heart. True religion rejoices in Christ (Jeremiah 9:23, 24; 1 Corinthians 1:30, 31). The word 'rejoice' has the idea of confident joy, or such confidence and faith as produces joy. We who believe, 'Rejoice in Christ Jesus'. We rejoice in his Person, in his work, in his Word, in his will, in his providence, in his promise, and in his love.

True religion is not outward but inward and spiritual. False religion is outward and carnal. True religion is a matter of the heart. It is the spiritual, heart worship of God (1 Samuel 16:7; Isaiah 66:1-4; John 4:24). True religion is a Person. False religion emphasizes things. True religion looks to Christ and rests in what he has done. False religion looks to and rests in what man has done. True religion has no confidence in the flesh; no, not in the experiences, emotions, or works of the flesh. Our complete confidence is in Christ, not in ourselves, but in Christ alone. True religion is a personal, living, and continual knowledge of Christ. Christ is the foundation, the centre, the sum, and the essence of all saving faith.

God's true servants, those who are called and sent of God to preach the true gospel, are not at all like the prophets of deceit. They are different in their motives and in their message. The test of every preacher is this: What does he preach?

I can tell you five things that will characterize the ministry of every man who is sent of God to preach the gospel:

1. He will preach that man is nothing but a loathsome mass of sin (Romans 3:9-19).
2. He will preach that God is a God of sovereign purpose and irresistible power (Romans 11:33-36).
3. He will preach Christ as an effectual Redeemer and prevailing Intercessor (Hebrews 10:11-14).
4. He will preach that the Holy Spirit is the Divine Giver and Preserver of life (John 6:63).
5. He will preach that all the fulness of grace and glory is in Christ (1 Corinthians 1:30).

I have warned you plainly of false religion. It is the greatest danger you will ever face. Give it no credibility and offer it no support. God our Father is a Spirit and he is seeking men to worship him in spirit and in truth. To worship him you must worship him in the truth of the gospel, you must worship him in your heart, and you must worship him by confident faith in Christ alone. In true religion, Christ is all!

Chapter 13

Who Are The True People Of God?

For we are the circumcision, which worship God in the spirit, and rejoice in Christ Jesus, and have no confidence in the flesh.

(Philippians 3:3)

There have always been certain religious groups which claimed to be the true church, the true people of God. They say if you are not of us, you are not among the Lord's true people. Who are God's true people?

The Jews claim to be God's true people because they are the physical seed of Abraham because they have been circumcised in the flesh. The Roman Catholics claim to be the true people of God because they claim that the church of Rome is the only true church. There are many others who claim that their church is the only true church, that apart from their church there is no true salvation. Who is right?

While we conscientiously adhere to those doctrines and practices which we believe to be true, we must avoid a proud, sectarian spirit. Yet, it is evident that not all who profess faith in Christ possess faith in Christ. It is one thing to be religious, it is another thing to be saved. It is one thing to be a part of a religious organization, it is something else to be in the church, the body of Christ. All that glitters is not gold, and 'they are not all Israel, which are of Israel' (Romans 9:6).

How can we know who are the true people of God? I do not raise the question so that you may examine others. I raise this question so that each one may examine himself. Am I one of the Lord's true people? How can I know whether or not I am one of God's elect? Not by what

I believe. Demas believed the truth. Not by what I practise in religion. Judas had the right form of religion. Not by what I do, or do not do. The Pharisees were meticulous, straight-laced and outwardly moral. Not by the great religious experiences I have had. Lot's wife had many great experiences.

Who are the true people of God? How can I know whether or not I am one of God's elect? Paul tells us, 'We are the circumcision, which worship God in the Spirit, and rejoice in Christ Jesus, and have no confidence in the flesh.'

In this one brief verse of Scripture, the Apostle Paul describes for us four distinct characteristics of God's elect.

Operation of grace

'We are the circumcision.' Every true believer has experienced an inward work of grace called the circumcision of the heart. If I am truly a believer, a child of God, I have experienced this mighty operation of divine grace in my heart (Romans 2:29). Often we refer to this operation of grace as 'the new birth', but it is described several ways in the New Testament. The new birth is a spiritual resurrection (John 5:24, 25). The new birth is a new creation (2 Corinthians 5:17). Here Paul speaks of the new birth as a spiritual circumcision of the heart (Colossians 2:10, 11).

In the Old Testament, God's covenant people were circumcised in the flesh. The cutting away of the flesh of the foreskin was a ceremonial picture of redemption and conversion, the circumcision of the heart. In circumcision, the filth of the flesh was cut away. In the new birth, the old man is cut off and Christ is formed in us. This circumcision of the heart is the work of God alone. It is made without hands, by the power of God. To be circumcised in my heart is to have my heart cut open by the hand of God and my inmost sin exposed to the eye of God. The knife which the Lord uses to circumcise the hearts of his people is the Word of God (Hebrews 4:12). Circumcision is the cutting off of the heart from every false hope.

Circumcision was the seal of God's covenant to Abraham (Genesis 17:9-11). The Holy Spirit is the seal of God's covenant to us in Christ (Ephesians 1:13, 14). Circumcision distinguished the Jews from the Gentiles. It was a mark of distinction, identifying and separating the children of Abraham from all others. The circumcision of the heart is a mark in the believer, identifying him as a child of God. It is not a mark seen by the eyes of men, but by the eyes of God alone (1 Samuel 16:7). The new birth is that act of grace by which all of God's elect are separated from the rest of mankind.

Circumcision was an act of cleansing in the flesh. The new birth is the purifying of the heart and conscience by the blood of Christ. Circumcision was a painful thing to endure. The new birth is attended with the painful conviction of the Holy Spirit. When Christ is revealed he will cause pain and contrition of heart (Zechariah 12:10).

Circumcision was a permanent work. The new birth is a permanent work of grace in the heart. Only God can speak to your heart. Only God can wound your heart. Only God can expose your sin and destroy your refuge of lies. To be circumcised in your heart is to have your heart pricked with a true sense of your sin, under Holy Spirit conviction. To be circumcised in your heart is to have your heart broken before God (Psalm 51:17; Isaiah 66:2). The hardness of the heart is removed when the iniquity of the heart is exposed. If ever you come under Holy Spirit conviction by a revelation of Christ in your heart, you will loathe your sin, you will know the shame of your sin, you will acknowledge your sin, and you will renounce all of your own supposed righteousness before God.

When Paul says, 'We are the circumcision', he is saying we are the true people of God; we are the true Israel of God; we are the church of God. Only those whose hearts have been circumcised by divine grace are born of God. If I am one of God's elect, I have experienced this mighty operation of grace in my heart.

Worship

'Which worship God in the Spirit.' Do we know anything about true worship (John 4:23, 24)? Do we know what it is to worship God in the Spirit? Public worship is important. We must not neglect it. But true worship is much more than going through the acts of worship. There are many who worship God publicly, who never worship God privately. Many who meticulously observe the externals of worship know nothing of internal worship. God's saints worship him.

Public worship is easily performed, but private worship is difficult. Public worship gains the approval of men, but private worship seeks the approval of God. Public worship may make a man proud and self-righteous, but private worship will humble a man before God. Public worship is pleasing to the flesh, but private worship brings peace and comfort to the heart. Public worship tells men what I want them to think I am, but private worship reveals what I really am.

True worship is not a physical act. We have no physical objects of worship. We have no physical help to worship. All physical worship is idolatry. All men are idolaters by nature. Therefore, idolatry is very appealing to the flesh. But God forbids it (Exodus 20:4, 5). God's saints all worship God in his true character! We worship God exclusively, carefully making certain that we render praise, honour, and glory to no one else.

God gave us his Son in the incarnation, through the womb of the virgin, but man passes by Christ and worships the virgin Mary. Christ died upon the cross to redeem us from sin, but man passes by Christ and worships the cross. Our Lord gave us the ordinance of baptism as a symbolic confession of faith in him, but man passes by Christ and makes baptism his saviour. Christ gave us the bread and wine of the Lord's Supper to remind us what he has done for us, but man passes by Christ and makes the bread and wine his saviour.

True worship is a spiritual act of the heart toward God. I cannot stress this enough. Worship is a matter of the heart. God looks upon the heart. We worship God because he is God. We worship God because he has been gracious to us in election, redemption, calling, and providence (Psalm 34:1-7). We worship God because he is a Father unto us and we are his sons and daughters.

What is true worship? True worship is a humble submission of the heart to the sovereign Lord. True worship is an adoring reverence of God. True worship is faith in God. It is the trust and confidence of the believing heart. True worship is praise and thanksgiving to God.

True worship is in the spirit. We worship God by the grace, the power, and the direction of the Holy Spirit. Idolaters have a carnal god who is impressed with carnal things. They worship with carnal things; images, robes, pictures, crosses, altars, and ceremonies. Those things which they call 'aids' to worship actually forbid worship (Hebrews 13:10). All carnal worship is a pretence, a show in the flesh, no more! Our worship is spiritual. It is a matter of the heart. We worship God according to the revelation of the Spirit. We worship God spiritually, personally, inwardly (Matthew 6:3, 4, 6, 17, 18). We worship him by the free, spontaneous exercise of faith, hope, and love toward him.

Rejoices

'Rejoice in Christ Jesus.' The word 'rejoice' here is not the same word that we had in verse 1 of chapter 3. The word 'rejoice' here has in it not only the idea of joy and happiness, but also of glorying, trusting, boasting, and confidence. What Paul tells us here is that all who are born of God, who have been circumcised in their hearts, who worship God in their hearts, confidently trust Christ alone for acceptance with God. The true believer is one who has a thankful sense of his Redeemer's mercy, and desires to praise him for it. We rejoice in Christ Jesus and glory in him as our all-sufficient Lord and Saviour. To rejoice in Christ is to glory in him as our All in all.

What is your glory and crown of rejoicing? Is it your religion? Is it your doctrinal creed? Is it your good character? Is it your wisdom? Or is it the Lord Jesus Christ? Every true believer rejoices in Christ alone (1 Corinthians 1:30, 31).

We rejoice in who Christ is. He is God our Saviour! We rejoice in Christ in all his offices. He is my Prophet to teach me. He is my Priest to redeem me. He is my King to rule over me.

We rejoice in what Christ has done; his suretyship engagements, his incarnation, his representative life, his substitutionary atonement, and his triumphant exaltation.

We rejoice in the fact that Christ is where he is, on the right hand of the majesty on high (Hebrews 8:1). Christ our High Priest sits upon the throne of heaven and makes intercession for us to God. He is the right man (Hebrews 7:21-25). He has done the right thing (Hebrews 9:11, 12, 20). He is in the right place (Hebrews 8:1). He offers the right plea (Hebrews 9:22; 1 John 2:1, 2).

We rejoice in all the blessings and privileges bestowed upon us in Christ (Ephesians 1:3). We rejoice in redemption, pardon, justification, acceptance, adoption, peace, and hope of eternal life.

We rejoice in Christ always. I cannot always rejoice in the events of my life, but I can always rejoice in Christ Jesus my Lord. In adversity as well as in prosperity, in sickness as in health, in sorrow and in joy, I can and will rejoice in Christ Jesus. To rejoice in Christ is to be content and satisfied with him. To rejoice in Christ is to say, Christ is enough (Psalm 73:25, 26). We will rejoice in Christ forever (Psalm 17:15).

No confidence in the flesh

'And have no confidence in the flesh.' The word 'flesh' means anything other than the Lord Jesus Christ which a man might look to as the basis of his acceptance with God. We place no confidence in our earthly privileges. We place no confidence in our religious experiences. We place no confidence in our church affiliation. We place no confidence in our service for Christ. We place no confidence in our good works. We place no confidence in our 'personal holiness'. Our only confidence before God is Christ. Charles Wesley wrote,

> Other refuge have I none,
> Hangs my helpless soul on Thee.

Christ alone is my confidence and hope for all things before God. He has given me a good, expectant, confident hope. Edward Mote wrote:

> My hope is built on nothing less
> Than Jesus' blood and righteousness.
> I dare not trust the sweetest frame,
> But wholly lean on Jesus' name.
> On Christ the solid Rock I stand,
> All other ground is sinking sand.

In Christ I am confident of God's approval and acceptance. In Christ I am confident of the resurrection. In Christ I am confident that I shall not be found wanting in the day of judgment. In Christ I am confident of my eternal inheritance in heaven.

> Jesus, thy blood and righteousness
> my beauty are, my glorious dress;
> 'midst flaming worlds, in these arrayed,
> with joy shall I lift up my head.

Bold shall I stand in thy great day;
for who aught to my charge shall lay?
Fully absolved through these I am
from sin and fear, from guilt and shame.

When from the dust of death I rise
to claim my mansion in the skies,
e'en then this shall be all my plea,
Jesus hath lived, hath died, for me.

Jesus, be endless praise to thee,
whose boundless mercy hath for me,
for me a full atonement made,
an everlasting ransom paid.

O let the dead now hear thy voice;
now bid thy banished ones rejoice;
their beauty this, their glorious dress,
Jesus, thy blood and righteousness.

Nicolaus Ludwig, Graf von Zinzendorf

Who are the true people of God? They have experienced a mighty operation of grace. They worship God in the Spirit. They rejoice in Christ Jesus. They have no confidence in the flesh.

Would you be numbered among the people of God? Bow down and worship God. Trust the Lord Jesus Christ. Renounce all your supposed righteousness. If you do these things, it is because the Lord himself has performed a mighty operation of grace in your heart. You, too, are among the circumcision, the true people of God.

Chapter 14

'That I May Win Christ'

Though I might also have confidence in the flesh. If any other man thinketh that he hath whereof he might trust in the flesh, I more: ... But what things were gain to me, those I counted loss for Christ. Yea doubtless, and I count all things but loss for the excellency of the knowledge of Christ Jesus my Lord: for whom I have suffered the loss of all things, and do count them but dung, that I may win Christ, and be found in him, not having mine own righteousness, which is of the law, but that which is through the faith of Christ, the righteousness which is of God by faith: That I may know him, and the power of his resurrection, and the fellowship of his sufferings, being made conformable unto his death; If by any means I might attain unto the resurrection of the dead ... Nevertheless, whereto we have already attained, let us walk by the same rule, let us mind the same thing.

(Philippians 3:4-16)

Most people today have a religion that says, 'Peace, peace, when there is no peace'. When they hear a man speak, like the Apostle Paul, of desiring to 'win Christ, and be found in him', they are conditioned to respond, 'I settled that issue a long time ago. I am never concerned about that matter. I have assurance of my salvation.'

I know that salvation is by grace alone. We are not saved by anything which we do. We trust the blood and righteousness of Christ alone for the whole of our acceptance before God. Yet, I know this, too, all true faith is persevering faith.

It is not the man who begins the race who wins the prize, but the man who finishes the race. It is not the man who begins in faith who is saved, but the man who dies in faith. That term, 'Once saved always saved', is misleading. As it is understood by most people, it is false. Many men and women have begun well and ended in hell. It is not enough to have believed. We must go on believing. It is not enough to profess faith. We must persevere in faith. The life of faith is the lifelong pursuit of Christ. We must know Christ today. How truly blessed is that man and that woman who can say with Paul, 'I count all things but loss … that I may win Christ'. Would you win Christ? Would you be found in him at the last day? If you would, the Apostle Paul tells us four things that must be done by us.

A renunciation that must be made
Paul shows us by example that self-denial is an essential aspect of saving faith. It is not a singular act of renouncing self. It is a perpetual, daily dying to self. Paul said, 'I die daily' (1 Corinthians 15:31). This is what he meant: for Christ's sake he renounced everything that had been dear to him. He counted all things but dung for Christ. For Paul, it was truly a costly thing to follow Christ, but he willingly, readily, and constantly paid the price.

The Lord Jesus Christ revealed himself to the Apostle Paul in a most extraordinary way on the Damascus Road. He revealed both his glorious Person and the glory of his grace toward sinners through the merits of his sin atoning death upon the cross. Paul never got over the wonder of it. His soul was consumed by the amazing grace and mercy of God. The great, life governing ambition of his renewed heart was that he might know Christ. Having seen the glory of Christ upon the cross, Paul renounced his former religion and his earthly advantages over other men and exchanged all his earthly riches and prospects for hunger, thirst, nakedness, peril, and bitter persecution. He counted his circumcision and his noble birth as useless things. And he renounced his worldly honour, his name, his reputation, his scholarly education, and his social distinction (vv. 7, 8). Everything that Paul had cherished and worked so hard to gain, everything that had been advantageous to him as a man in this world, he renounced as rubbish, and continued to renounce as rubbish. Thirty years later, he had no regrets.

If you and I would have Christ, we must do the same thing that Paul did. What does it cost to be a Christian? It will cost you everything you have. 'He that loveth father or mother more than me is not worthy of me: and he that taketh not his cross, and followeth after me, is not worthy of me. He that findeth his life shall lose it: and he that loseth his life for my sake shall find it' (Matthew 10:37-39). 'Whosoever he be of you that forsaketh not all that he hath, he cannot be my disciple' (Luke 14:33).

The life of faith begins in self-denial. The life of faith is a life of perpetual self-denial. The life of faith is an increasing self-denial. 'I beseech you therefore, brethren, by the mercies of God, that ye present your bodies a living sacrifice, holy, acceptable unto God, which is your reasonable service. And be not conformed to this world: but be ye transformed by the renewing of your mind, that ye may prove what is that good, and acceptable, and perfect will of God' (Romans 12:1, 2).

A reward that must be sought
Paul tells us there is a good reason for complete self-denial, and that there is a reward that must be sought. Remember, these are the words of a believer. Paul is telling us why he continually denied himself and daily died to this world. He said, I count all things but loss, because I am seeking something far better. He said, I have counted the cost, and I am ready to do whatever it takes to have Christ. 'Yea, doubtless, and I count all things but loss for the excellency of the knowledge of Christ Jesus my Lord: for whom I have suffered the loss of all things, and do count them but dung, that I may win Christ.'

We are thankful for family, friends, health, and the many comforts of life with which we are blessed; but we must have Christ. This is the one thing that we want as believers above all other things. This is our one consuming desire, 'That I may win Christ'. We must not be satisfied merely to be religious, moral, and respectable. We must truly be in Christ, united to him by faith, living in union with him, one with Christ. We must 'win Christ and be found in him'.

'That I may know him.' This was the desire of Paul's heart, and it is the desire of my heart. Our Lord said, 'This is life eternal, that they might know thee the only true God, and Jesus Christ, whom thou hast sent' (John 17:3). There is one thing alone which we need for our eternal salvation, our growth in grace, and our everlasting happiness;

that one thing is the knowledge of Christ. To know him is to live. To know him is salvation. Not to know him is to perish. Not to know him is damnation.

Many people know the history of Christ, but few know Christ himself. Many admire his way among men, but do not see him as the Way. Many people know the moral example of Christ, but few know Christ. Many people know the doctrine of Christ's atonement, but few people know Christ who is our Atonement. Many people know the doctrine of Christ's salvation, but few people know Christ who is our Salvation. Many people know the doctrine of Christ's Lordship, but few people know Christ the Lord. Salvation is not knowing about Christ. Salvation is knowing Christ. Paul's great heart's desire was that he might know the Lord Jesus Christ. And this is my heart's desire and the heart's desire of all those redeemed by the blood of Christ, 'That I may know him'.

Everything I know of Christ, everything I have experienced of God's saving grace, everything I know about the gospel continually compels me, by the power and grace of God the Holy Spirit, to seek these three goals, three goals for which I labour: total commitment to Christ, total communion with Christ, and total conformity to Christ. I want to bring honour and glory to my God and Saviour. I want to surrender everything to him. Begone all self-ambition! Begone all self-motivation! Begone all self-desire! Begone all self-seeking! Let me live for Christ alone! My heart longs to know Christ's presence, fellowship, and direction at all times. The very thought of pure, uninterrupted, free communion with Christ at all times fills my heart with bliss. I want to be like my Redeemer in thought, in word, and in deed. Like him; full of love, kindness, and tenderness. Like him; thoughtful, generous, considerate. Like him, without sin.

We want to live above this world, above its cares, above this place of death and decay. 'If ye then be risen with Christ, seek those things which are above, where Christ sitteth on the right hand of God. Set your affection on things above, not on things on the earth. For ye are dead, and your life is hid with Christ in God' (Colossians 3:1-3). We want to be like Christ in heart, in spirit, in attitude, and in conduct. My heart is greatly concerned and burdened about many things as they relate to the glory of God, the gospel of God, the will of God, and the people of God. But all the great burdens of my heart can be briefly summarized and expressed in these five words, 'That I may know him'. This is the reward I am seeking. This is the reward which all true believers seek.

We want to know the riches of our Saviour's grace; his eternal grace, his redeeming grace, his pardoning grace, his regenerating grace, his preserving grace, and his providential grace (Ephesians 1:3). We want to know the love of Christ that passes knowledge. 'That Christ may dwell in your hearts by faith; that ye, being rooted and grounded in love, may be able to comprehend with all saints what is the breadth, and length, and depth, and height; and to know the love of Christ, which passeth knowledge, that ye might be filled with all the fulness of God' (Ephesians 3:17-19).

'That I may know him, and the power of his resurrection.' The resurrection of our Lord Jesus was a marvellous display of divine power. Our Lord said, concerning his life, 'I have power to lay it down, and I have power to take it again'. He was Master over death, even when it appeared that death had mastered him. He entered the grave as a captive, but he arose from the tomb as Conqueror. His resurrection tells us that Christ's work of redemption was finished. His resurrection was God's public declaration that our sins had been put away by the sacrifice of his darling Son and that we are justified (Romans 4:25; Hebrews 9:26). The penalty of sin was fully paid (Hebrews 9:12). When he arose from the dead, we arose in him representatively. The new birth is a resurrection from spiritual death to spiritual life in Christ (1 Peter 1:3). It is accomplished in us by that same power that raised Christ from the dead (Ephesians 1:19, 20). The power of his resurrection guarantees that we, too, will be raised in the last day (1 Corinthians 15:47-49).

Paul is also referring here to the spiritual influence of Christ's resurrection in our hearts. We want to know Christ who is the resurrection. We want to walk in this world, just as our Lord did, as resurrected men and women, in newness of life. 'Therefore we are buried with him by baptism into death: that like as Christ was raised up from the dead by the glory of the Father, even so we also should walk in newness of life. For if we have been planted together in the likeness of his death, we shall be also in the likeness of his resurrection' (Romans 6:4, 5). 'Likewise reckon ye also yourselves to be dead indeed unto sin, but alive unto God through Jesus Christ our Lord' (Romans 6:11). I want to know the power of Christ's resurrection, exaltation, and sovereign rule that I may trust his wise, unerring providence in all things (Romans 8:28).

'That I may know him ... and the fellowship of his sufferings.' No man can enter into the agony that the Son of God endured upon the cursed tree when he was made sin for us. He died so that we might never know the torments he endured! But we want to know all we can of what Christ suffered for us in order to redeem us. We want to know what our Saviour suffered in the Garden of Gethsemane and what he suffered on the cross. We want to know his bodily anguish, his mental anguish, and his soul's agony for us. We want to share the reproach he endured for us. We want to know the benefits of Christ's sufferings for us; our justification, reconciliation, pardon, peace, and eternal salvation. I pray that God will give me grace to willingly bear the reproach of Christ in this world as he willingly bore my reproach before God, and that he will keep me from doing anything to shelter myself from suffering reproach for his name's sake.

'Being made conformable unto his death; If by any means I might attain unto the resurrection of the dead.' With the Apostle Paul, we, too, want to be transformed into the likeness of Christ and conformed to his death; in total surrender, in total self-denial, in total sacrifice, in total commitment. We want to have such a true and intimate knowledge of Christ that we may be like him in all things. As we have been crucified with Christ, let us die with him daily. Let us die to self, to sin, and to this world, having the affections and lusts of the flesh crucified and the deeds of the body mortified. As he willingly laid down his life for us, let us willingly lay down our life for him (Acts 20:24).

We do not desire conformity to religious tradition. We do not seek conformity to human opinion. We do not seek conformity to the law of Moses, written upon tables of stone. We seek conformity to Christ in his death. Let us seek conformity to Christ in his death such that our meat and drink is to do his will, to count his cause our cause, and to be willing to do or suffer anything for his name's sake.

A race that must be run
Paul was a saved man. He rejoiced in Christ Jesus and had no confidence in the flesh. He knew he was redeemed, justified, forgiven of all sin, and complete in Christ. Yet, Paul was a man in a state of conscious imperfection. He says, 'Not as though I had already attained,

either were already perfect'. This man knew his sin, and he despised it. He knew the weakness and imperfections of the flesh. It caused him to cry from the depths of his soul, 'O wretched man that I am! Who shall deliver me from the body of this death?' Paul's awareness of his sin made him struggle hard against it. With the full awareness of his sin, indeed, because of that awareness, he was constantly pressing forward. 'But I follow after, if that I may apprehend that for which also I am apprehended of Christ Jesus.'

We do not use this word 'apprehend' very often. In fact, I can only think of one common usage of it. When we speak of a policeman arresting a criminal, we say, 'The fugitive has been apprehended'. He has been seized, grabbed, laid hold of, arrested. That is exactly Paul's meaning. Paul had been apprehended by God's almighty grace on the Damascus Road. Grace grabbed him! That is how God saves sinners. Paul always felt the grasp that Christ had upon him. He never got away from it. It was a life-long grasp. With Paul, this arrest by Christ was the force and motive by which his life was directed, and governed for the rest of his days.

Like Paul, we who believe were apprehended by Christ. We were running from the Lord. We were like lost sheep, within the reach of the wolf, when the Lord Jesus stepped in and laid hold on us. Almighty grace laid hold on us, and we could not escape the hand of mercy. We surrendered ourselves as captives under the dominion of Christ.

As the Apostle Paul drew near the end of his pilgrimage, even as he was finishing his course, he said, 'Brethren, I count not myself to have apprehended: but this one thing I do'. Paul was single-minded, governed by 'one thing'. Being governed by just 'one thing', he pressed on toward the goal for the prize of the upward call of God in Christ Jesus. What was that 'one thing' always in the forefront of Paul's mind, the 'one thing' which kept him motivated and inspired, the 'one thing' he just had to have? It was the perfection of resurrection glory, the consummation of the high calling of God in Christ Jesus. Blessed are those people who are occupied with 'one thing', if that one thing is Christ.

'Forgetting those things which are behind, and reaching forth unto those things which are before, I press toward the mark for the prize of the high calling of God in Christ Jesus.' The Apostle Paul once wrote of himself as 'the least of the apostles', one not worthy to be called an apostle, because he persecuted the church of God (1 Corinthians 15:9). He spoke of himself later as 'less than the least of all saints' (Ephesians 3:8). And when he was an old man, ready to leave this world, he said he was the chief of sinners (1 Timothy 1:15). Thirty years later, he was still astonished that Christ had poured out his life's blood unto death to redeem him. Paul never forgot what he was and where he was when God sought him out and saved him by his grace. He never let himself forget that he had proudly blasphemed Christ and persecuted the church; but that all was behind him, covered by the blood of the Redeemer. He was never governed by his past. He did not erase his past from his memory, but his past did not rule over him with gloom, or hamper his present usefulness.

We must not trust in any measure those things which we have experienced. We place no confidence in the flesh. 'Forgetting those things which are behind.' Forgetting past works, past usefulness, past triumphs, past steadfastness, past weaknesses, and past failures. We rather strive for those things set before us; the promises of the gospel, the blessings of grace, the knowledge of Christ. Let us ever be found pressing on, never looking back, never stepping aside, never quitting, always pressing on 'toward the mark for the prize of the high calling of God in Christ Jesus' (v. 14).

Children of God, the past is the past! That is how God views it, and it is how God would have us view it! Do not dwell on it, and do not act as if your transgressions are greater than God's grace!

May God the Holy Spirit constantly bring to our memories his marvellous, amazing grace in delivering our souls from bondage, and thereby melt our hearts before the throne of grace. Nothing will stir up our hearts and minds so effectively, nothing can motivate and govern our lives better than the remembrance of redemption and grace in and by the Lord Jesus Christ.

'Reaching forth unto those things which are before.' The life of faith is aptly compared to runners in a race. Here Paul is inspiring us, exhorting us, and alluring us to run with him in the race of faith. The race that is set before us requires diligence, perseverance, and commitment (Hebrews 12:1-4, 12-17).

Paul knew the Saviour, probably more fully and clearly than any man who ever lived upon the earth. He knew he had a saving interest in Christ. Yet, he knew his knowledge was only partial, imperfect knowledge, therefore, he desired to know Christ more fully, more intimately, more completely. He wanted to know all he could of Christ. His soul could never be satisfied with anything less than the perfect knowledge of his beloved Redeemer. On the earth, such perfect knowledge is unattainable. But Paul pressed toward the mark of perfect knowledge. He sought it with all his heart. Paul seems to have almost forgotten every other concern and addicted himself to this one object, 'I press toward the mark for the prize of the high calling of God in Christ Jesus.'

Let us press toward the mark that we might know Christ. To know his love, his sufferings, his power, and to know Christ himself. Let us press toward the mark that we might be conformed to Christ. Let us be conformed to his will, his example, and his image. This must be the all-consuming ambition of our heart, 'That I may win Christ and be found in him'.

This is my goal. I want to finish my course with joy, that I may win the supreme, heavenly prize, 'that I may win Christ'. 'As for me, I will behold thy face in righteousness: I shall be satisfied, when I awake, with thy likeness' (Psalm 17:15). 'Beloved, now are we the sons of God, and it doeth not yet appear what we shall be: but we know that, when he shall appear, we shall be like him; for we shall see him as he is. And every man that hath this hope in him purifieth himself, even as he is pure' (1 John 3:2, 3). Pressing toward that mark, when my life's journey is over, when my race is run, I shall have, by the grace of God, that which I seek after; total commitment to Christ, total communion with Christ, and total conformity to Christ. Oh, what a blessed hope we have in Christ!

A rule that must be followed
If we would run this race and win this prize, there is a rule that must be followed. We must live by faith in Christ. We must walk in those paths of gospel truth which God has revealed to us. We must run the race, 'Looking unto Jesus, the Author and Finisher of our faith' (Hebrews 12:2).

'Let us therefore, as many as be perfect, be thus minded' (v.15). All who are taught of God have this attitude and hold these convictions. They denounce their own righteousness and seek the righteousness of Christ. They want Christ above all things. They seek Christ above all things. The more we know of Christ, the more loathsome and abhorrent we become in our own eyes (Job 40:3-5; 42:5, 6; Isaiah 6:15; Psalm 51:1-5), and the more we see the all-sufficiency of Christ. The more we know of him, the more we realize how much we need the blood of Christ to cleanse us, the righteousness of Christ to clothe us, the strength of Christ to support us, the advocacy of Christ to plead for us, and the grace of Christ to preserve us.

'Let us walk by the same rule, let us mind the same thing.' As we anticipate the days that may yet be appointed for us, let us be found walking with God, walking in the steps of faith, trusting Christ. Whatever degree of the knowledge of Christ and whatever light we have in gospel truth, we are responsible to walk in it. As we walk in the light God gives us, he will give us more light.

By these things, we may examine ourselves and see whether or not we are in the faith. Do I count all things loss for Christ? Do I desire above all things to know Christ and be like Christ? Do I strive after this knowledge of and likeness to Christ? Am I looking to Christ for all things, resting my soul upon him? Hymnwriter Robert Robinson said,

> Here I raise mine Ebenezer,
> Hither by Thy help I've come;
> And I hope by Thy good pleasure
> Safely to arrive at home.

The race finished
The reward of faith is Christ himself. All who finish the race shall receive a full, complete reward. None shall be disappointed. 'Thou wilt show me the path of life: in thy presence is fulness of joy; and at thy right hand there are pleasures for evermore' (Psalm 16:11). 'As for me, I will behold Thy face in righteousness: I shall be satisfied, when I awake with thy likeness' (Psalm 17:15).

Fix your eyes upon Christ and press on toward the goal. Set your heart on him. Do you want him more than anything? Are you hungry for him? Does your heart beat for him? Then lay aside everything that would hinder you and run, run, run, that you may win Christ and be found in him! There is but one thing in the world really worth pursuing, and that one thing is the knowledge of Christ!

Lift up the hands that hang down, strengthen the feeble knees, press onward, press forward. Let us run with patience the race that is set before us, and when the race is over, we shall have the prize which we have sought for so long. We shall obtain total commitment to Christ. We shall obtain total communion with Christ. We shall obtain total conformity to Christ.

Chapter 15

'Enemies Of The Cross Of Christ'

Brethren, be followers together of me, and mark them which walk so as ye have us for an ensample. (For many walk, of whom I have told you often, and now tell you even weeping, that they are the enemies of the cross of Christ: Whose end is destruction, whose God is their belly, and whose glory is in their shame, who mind earthly things.)

(Philippians 3:17-19)

A faithful pastor has many responsibilities. As I stand before eternity-bound sinners to preach the gospel of Christ week after week, there are several things which I must do. If I would be faithful to the Lord my God who has called me, faithful to the Holy Scriptures, faithful to the souls of men, and faithful to my own conscience, I must give myself whole-heartedly to these things. I must seek God's message for the hour; and I must boldly deliver that message, considering neither men's approval or their disapproval of it.

The faithful servant of God must preach the gospel with simplicity and clarity. He must instruct the people of God in doctrinal truth. Christ's sheep must be fed with knowledge and understanding. Sometimes God's servant must deliver a message of reproof and rebuke for the discipline of God's family. The discipline of the church is to be done in the pulpit.

God's servants must endeavour to comfort and encourage the people of God in the faith of the gospel. At times the people of God must be challenged and stirred with regard to their responsibilities. Sometimes the people of God simply need to have their hearts warmed and cheered. And the faithful servant of God must sometimes sound a word of solemn warning.

I know some people get upset when a preacher warns a congregation in plain terms about false prophets, false doctrine, and false religion. But if I am to faithfully watch over the souls of men, as one who must give account, I dare not keep silent about 'the enemies of the cross'.

The men whom Paul describes as 'the enemies of the cross of Christ' were teachers and preachers in the church at Philippi. They claimed to be true believers. They claimed that they were the servants of Christ. They claimed to be preaching the gospel of Christ. I have no doubt that these men preached what we call 'the fundamentals of the faith'. They preached the inspiration of the Bible, the virgin birth, the death, burial, and resurrection of Christ, and the second coming of Christ. Yet, Paul calls these men, 'the enemies of the cross of Christ: whose end is destruction'.

Paul spoke in plain terms about these cunning, crafty, seducers, who made merchandise of the souls of men, not because he was a bitter antagonist, who loved a good fight, but because he was devoted to the glory of God, the gospel of Christ, and the souls of men.

These men at Philippi were bitterly opposed to Paul, and vehemently opposed to the gospel of the grace of God which he preached. They did everything they could to discredit Paul and to mar the beauty of the gospel. The way they did it was to raise a smoke screen and a cloud of dust, falsely accusing him of many evil things.

They accused Paul of being a false apostle and an antinomian. They accused him of being a divider of men. These accusations were made by these false prophets in an attempt to hide the one real issue. They themselves were 'the enemies of the cross of Christ'. They hated the God whom Paul proclaimed. They hated the Christ he preached. They hated the gospel message of the cross.

Things are no different in our day. The church of Christ is plagued today, as never before, with men in her pulpits who are 'the enemies of the cross of Christ'. They rebel against the preaching of the gospel, and they despise those who preach it. They raise many false issues and make many false accusations against those who preach the gospel of God's free and sovereign grace in Christ, as an excuse for their own rebellion to the Word of God. By their many false accusations they are attempting to excuse, or at least to cover over, their own heart-enmity toward the cross of our Lord Jesus Christ. These are only smoke screens, raised to hide the real issue. The real issue is just this, they are 'the enemies of the cross of Chris'. The cross of Christ is a stone of stumbling and a rock of offence to them. And what causes such great uproar and bitter antagonism among devoutly religious people is simply the doctrine of the cross.

In Philippians 3:18, 19, the Apostle Paul weeps as he warns the church of God about 'the enemies of the cross of Christ'. The messenger of Christ in tears delivers the solemn warning. Yet, the enemies of Christ are unmoved; pretending to be his friends, they are full of hostility toward him. Here is a preacher so heartbroken he weeps, and a congregation with hearts so hard that, though he told them the truth again and again, they do not regard it.

What is the cross of Christ which men vehemently oppose?
Paul tells us that 'the preaching of the cross is to them that perish foolishness'. He tells us that there are many who reject the gospel because of 'the offence of the cross'. Yet, men and women talk about the cross all the time. They sing about the cross. They wear crosses around their necks. They put crosses on top of their church buildings. What then is that cross of which Paul speaks when he says, 'They are the enemies of the cross of Christ'?

When Paul speaks of the cross, he is talking about the doctrine of the atonement. Man is not at all offended by the fact that God's Son died upon a Roman cross. But the enmity of man's heart is evident when you begin to proclaim the doctrine of the cross, the doctrine of the atonement which our Lord accomplished on the cross.

Those who oppose the doctrine of the atonement are 'the enemies of the cross of Christ'. Those who accept the atonement and rest their souls upon it are the friends of the cross. Here are four words that describe the doctrine of the cross and the work of our Lord Jesus Christ upon the cross.

Sovereignty
'The Good Shepherd giveth his life for the sheep' (John 10:11). Throughout the ordeal of his crucifixion and death our Saviour

displayed his total sovereignty as God. Never was he the helpless victim of circumstances. He voluntarily laid down his life for us.

Substitution (Isaiah 53:4-10)
Our Lord Jesus Christ died as a Substitute in our place. Bearing our sins in his body on the tree, he died in our place.

Success (Isaiah 42:4)
All that the Lord Jesus Christ intended to accomplish in his death, he has accomplished. All that he intended to do, he has done. All that he tried to perform, he has performed.

Satisfaction (Isaiah 53:11)
The death of our Lord Jesus Christ was an infinitely satisfactory atonement for sin. There is complete satisfaction in his blood. His blood satisfied the decrees of the Father, the demands of the law, the declarations of the prophets, and the desire of his people.

Those who are 'the enemies of the cross' try to belittle our Lord's great work of redemption. They make it out to be a very small thing. They teach that the Son of God did something or other, which in some way or other, in some measure or other, is connected with our redemption. But to assert that the Lord Jesus Christ has effectually accomplished the redemption of his people is most offensive to them.

When Paul talks about the cross of Christ, he is talking about the gospel message of the cross (2 Corinthians 5:18-21). This message declares:

1. Free forgiveness of sin through the blood of Christ (1 John 1:9).
2. Salvation by grace alone (Ephesians 2:8, 9).
3. Justification by faith alone (Romans 5:1). This is the theme of the Bible. 'The just shall live by faith.' This makes the gospel good news. This is the cause of every martyr's blood, from Abel down to this day. No man's blood was ever shed for preaching salvation by works. This was the theme of the reformation; grace alone, faith alone, Christ alone. This is the only hope for a sinner, the only assurance for a believer, and the only comfort for a dying man.
4. Acceptance in a Substitute (Ephesians 1:6). The Lord Jesus Christ has stood, is standing, and shall forever more stand before God as our

Substitute. In him we have no condemnation (Romans 8:1). In him we have no sin and are righteous (1 John 3:5).

Sometimes in the Scriptures the cross refers to that life which is the result of faith in Christ (Matthew 10:38, 39). The way of the cross is a life of self-denial. The true believer cannot, he will not, he dare not, live for himself, either in the accumulating of wealth, or the getting of fame, or the enjoyment of pleasure.

The way of the cross is a life of submission, surrender, and dedication to Christ as Lord. We are submissive to his will. We surrender to his authority. We are dedicated to his glory.

Those who are 'the enemies of the cross' rebel against the claims of Christ upon their lives. His yoke is a gall to their shoulders. They will not have it.

Why are some people the enemies of the cross of Christ?
What is there about the preaching of the cross which evokes such enmity and hostility from men and women? What is there in the preaching of the cross which is so offensive to them? People are not opposed to religion. They are not opposed to the idea of eternal salvation. Why then are some 'the enemies of the cross of Christ'?

The cross of Christ is opposed to the pride and dignity of man. The doctrine of the cross is humiliating. It leaves nothing for man to boast of or glory in. The cross stands as a vivid emblem of man's hatred of God. The cross of Christ is a clear reminder and portrayal of human sin. It destroys all human notions of human ability, human merit, and self-salvation. The cross of Christ makes man's religion, man's works, man's traditions, man's customs, man's moral dignity and self-righteousness a heap of rubbish.

The cross of Christ is offensive to men because its simplicity is opposed to human wisdom. The cross of Christ is a most unaccommodating doctrine. It will not bend to man's prejudice. It will not bow to man's passions. It will not give space for man's goodness. It will not allow room for man's wisdom. The gospel of Christ must be revealed. Otherwise, man will perish in his intellectual foolishness.

The cross of Christ evokes man's wrath and enmity because it puts all men and women on one level. All who enter heaven must enter by the same Door. All who go to glory must go in the same Way. Harlots and queens, drunkards and educators, whoremongers and moralists are all the same in the eyes of God. All are sinners. And there is but one place of cleansing for sinners, the cross of Christ.

The cross of Christ is offensive to men and women because it demands total surrender. God has set the terms of peace before you. He will never alter them. He demands total surrender to Christ. The cross of Christ is offensive because it shuts all up to Christ alone.

Who are the enemies of the cross of Christ?

Paul tell us that they are those men and women 'whose god is their belly, and whose glory is in their shame, who mind earthly things'. The enemies of the cross are people who live for self. 'Whose god is their belly'. The enemies of the cross are people who are shamefully proud. 'Whose glory is their shame.' The enemies of the cross are people who live for this world. 'Who mind earthly things.'

Some who are the enemies of the cross are in the pulpits of our churches. They preach for profit; they preach for personal gain; they preach for love of ease. Therefore, they endeavour to alter the doctrine of the cross. They do not out and out deny the cross. They simply alter its doctrines to accommodate their hearers.

They preach sovereignty, but not total sovereignty. They preach about sins, but never sin, or total depravity. They preach redemption, but not effectual, accomplished redemption. They preach grace, but not free, sovereign, irresistible grace.

Some who are the enemies of the cross of Christ are in the pews of our churches. These people whom Paul describes as 'enemies of the cross of Christ' were members of a church which he had started. They were professed Christians. They were outwardly and by profession moral, religious people. But in reality, in their hearts, they were 'the enemies of the cross of Christ'.

While they believed the doctrine of the cross in their heads, it had no effect upon their hearts. While they talked about the cross on Sunday, it had no power over their lives. While they held to the doctrine of the cross, they lived for the world. Their religion was only a profession. There was no self-denial, no sacrifice, no dedication, and no commitment to the cross.

What becomes of those who are 'the enemies of the cross of Christ'?
Paul describes the enemies of the cross as men and women 'whose end is destruction'. Their profession will be destroyed. All their hopes will be destroyed. All their happiness will be destroyed. In the end, they themselves will be destroyed.

How should we act before the enemies of the cross?
There is but one thing for us to do. We must go on preaching 'the cross of Christ'. The more I see man's enmity toward the cross, the more I am compelled to preach the doctrine of the cross. Those points of gospel truth which are most offensive to carnal men shall be my most constant theme.

I will proclaim God's absolute, total, and universal sovereignty. I will declare the total depravity, guilt, and inability of Adam's race. I will proclaim God's unconditional election of his people in Christ. I will preach the blessed gospel doctrine of limited, effectual atonement by the blood of Christ. I will declare that salvation is accomplished by the irresistible grace of God the Holy Spirit. I will preach the certain final perseverance and preservation of God's elect in Christ.

Ours is the gospel of grace; pure grace, eternal grace, sovereign grace, immutable grace, effectual grace, saving grace through the cross of Christ. Let us hold high the blood-stained banner and preach the cross in all its power and glory.

Chapter 16

'They Are Not Of The World'

For our conversation is in heaven; from whence also we look for the Saviour, the Lord Jesus Christ: Who shall change our vile body, that it may be fashioned like unto his glorious body, according to the working whereby he is able even to subdue all things unto himself.

(Philippians 3:20, 21)

Our Lord Jesus Christ says concerning all of his elect, 'They are not of the world, even as I am not of the world' (John 17:14, 16). In making that statement, our Lord is telling us that his people are strangers and pilgrims in the earth. True believers are not like those men and women who are of the world. God's elect live by different principles. The children of God live for different objects. Their motives, goals, interests, and ambitions are altogether different from those of other people. They are in the world, by reason of necessity, and they make the best use of their time here; but 'they are not of the world'.

To use the language of Holy Scripture, 'Here we have no continuing city', but we desire a better country, that is an heavenly. We do not look upon anything in this world as permanent. We recognize all earthly things and all earthly relationships are temporary. 'While we look not at the things which are seen, but at the things which are not seen: for the things which are seen are temporal; but the things which are not seen are eternal. For we know that if our earthly house of this tabernacle were dissolved, we have a building of God, an house not made with hands, eternal in the heavens' (2 Corinthians 4:18-5:1). Because the

127

people of God are not of the world, even as Christ our Lord was not of the world, 'the world knoweth us not, because it knew him not' (1 John 3:1).

These are the things Paul is dealing with in our text. 'For our conversation is in heaven; from whence also we look for the Saviour, the Lord Jesus Christ: Who shall change our vile body, that it may be fashioned like unto his glorious body, according to the working whereby he is able to subdue all things unto himself.' The people of God are strangers and pilgrims on this earth making their way to heaven, living in hope of a glorious change.

The believer's holy conversation

'For our conversation is in heaven.' Paul uses the word 'conversation' when he is talking about our manner of speech, our manner of life, the way we live. He is saying, God's people live in this world as men and women whose homeland is heaven.

Holiness of life for the children of God is not some kind of super pious show of outward religion. Holiness is not a certain manner of speech, a certain way of dress, or certain practices and customs of life. Holiness is sanctification to the Lord. It is commitment and dedication, and faithfulness of the heart to Christ. All of God's people lead holy lives. They are men and women whose hearts are attached not to this world, but to heaven. This is what Paul says, 'Our conversation is in heaven'.

Philip Doddridge gave this paraphrase of the text, 'But we converse as citizens of heaven, considering ourselves as citizens of the New Jerusalem, and only strangers and pilgrims on earth.'

Certainly Paul means for us to understand that we are strangers, aliens, and foreigners in this world (Hebrews 11:8-10, 16). Since we are aliens in this world, we must behave as such. We must be careful that we do not bring reproach upon our homeland. We want to do as much good as possible among those people with whom we dwell. We must not greatly concern ourselves with the affairs of this land. We are simply passing through this land. We must not yoke ourselves to its affairs. We are not eligible for the honours of this land. It would be very foolish for us to hoard up this world's treasures (Matthew 6:19-21).

Paul would have us constantly realize we are citizens of heaven. We are under heaven's government. Christ, the King of heaven, reigns in our hearts. The laws of glory are the laws of our consciences. Our daily prayer is, 'Thy will be done in earth, as it is in heaven'. The Spirit of God holds sway over our hearts. Grace reigns through righteousness in our souls. We gladly wear the easy yoke of our Master.

As citizens, we have a common right to all the property of heaven. It has been purchased for us by blood, earned for us by perfect righteousness, and claimed for us by a Substitute (Hebrews 6:20).

As citizens of the New Jerusalem, we share all of heaven's great honours (1 John 3:1). We are princes with God. We wear the robe of righteousness. Saints are our companions. Christ is our Brother. God is our Father.

Even now we enjoy the delights of our homeland. Do the saints in heaven rejoice over sinners that are born of God, over prodigals who come home? So do we. Do they chant the glories of triumphant grace? We do the same. Do they cast their crowns down at Immanuel's feet? All the honours we have, we cast at his feet, too. Do they rejoice in him? We do, too. Do they sing, 'Worthy is the Lamb'? Our hearts join their song. Yes, even though we are here upon the earth, our great joy is to know that our names are written in heaven.

Let us live in this world as people who are citizens of heaven (Colossians 3:1-3). It is a privilege for me to live in this land of peace, liberty, and prosperity. I would rather be a citizen of the United States of America than to be a citizen of any other country in the world. But the privilege of being a citizen of this country places upon me certain necessary obligations and responsibilities. Similarly, being a citizen of heaven, I have certain responsibilities to which I must be faithful.

It is my responsibility to seek the glory of God in all things and above all things and to seek the will of God. It is my responsibility to labour for the furtherance of the gospel. It is my responsibility to serve the interests of Christ's church and kingdom. Let me live not for this world, but for Christ. 'Love not the world' (Matthew 6:31-33).

> This is not my place of resting,
> Mine's a city yet to come;
> Onward to it I am hasting,
> On to my eternal home.

In it all is light and glory;
O'er it shines a nightless day;
Every trace of sin's sad story,
All the curse, hath passed away.

There the Lamb, our Shepherd leads us,
By the streams of life along,
On the freshest pastures feeds us,
Turns our sighing into song.

Soon we pass this desert dreary,
Soon we bid farewell to pain:
Never more are sad or weary,
Never, never sin again!

Horatius Bonar

The believer's confidence

'From whence also we look for the Saviour, the Lord Jesus Christ.' This is our blessed hope. Our Saviour, the Lord Jesus Christ, is coming again! We are looking for, expecting, and hastening unto the glorious appearing of the great God and our Saviour, Jesus Christ (Job 19:25-27; John 14:1-3; 1 Thessalonians 4:13-18; Titus 2:11-14).

Our Lord is coming to gather his own elect. He is coming to judge the earth. He is coming to establish his kingdom and glory in the earth.

The believer's heavenly change

Paul tells us that when our Lord returns, he will accomplish the believer's heavenly change. Our Saviour, the Lord Jesus Christ, is coming to this earth again; and when he does, he is that One, 'who shall change our vile body, that it may be fashioned like unto his glorious body, according to the working whereby he is able to subdue all things unto himself'.

When our Saviour comes, he will deliver us from the final results of sin. He will completely vindicate his people and bestow upon us the glorious inheritance of the saints in light.

He will 'change our vile body'. This earthly shell is the body of our humiliation. It is a temporary house for our souls. By reason of sin, it is called 'our vile body'. It is a body defiled by sin. It is a body attended with frailty. It is a body of mortality. It is a body that must soon die and be sown in the earth and return to dust.

But on the resurrection morning, this vile body shall be stripped of all its vileness. It shall be changed like unto the glorious body of Christ. 'As we have borne the image of the earthy, we shall also bear the image of the heavenly' (1 Corinthians 15:49). See Romans 8:29; 1 John 3:2.

The nature of the great change to take place in this vile body in the resurrection is clearly described for us in 1 Corinthians 15:42-58. It will be changed from corruption to incorruption, dishonour to glory, weakness to power, natural to spiritual. This resurrection will be universal. It will be instantaneous. It will be by the power of Christ.

The Lord Jesus Christ our Saviour is able to accomplish this great change. What he has promised he is able to perform. If he can subject all things, the totality of all the power of the universe, to himself, he certainly has the power to change our vile body that it may be fashioned like unto his glorious body.

He has put away sin by the sacrifice of himself. He has broken the power of Satan. He has governed the universe in perfect conformity to the will and glory of God. He has subdued the hearts of his people. He has broken the power of death. He has the power to raise the dead.

Let us live in this world as citizens of heaven. Let us live in anticipation of our Redeemer's return. Let us live in hope of the resurrection.

Chapter 17

'Rejoice In The Lord'

Therefore, my brethren dearly beloved and longed for, my joy and crown, so stand fast in the Lord, my dearly beloved. I beseech Euodias, and beseech Syntyche, that they be of the same mind in the Lord. And I intreat thee also, true yokefellow, help those women which laboured with me in the gospel, with Clement also, and with other my fellowlabourers, whose names are in the book of life. Rejoice in the Lord alway: and again I say, Rejoice.

(Philippians 4:1-4)

Let us remember that this exhortation is given by Paul when he was in prison at Rome, with iron fetters on his wrists. This exhortation is given to us by a man who had been slandered by his pretended friends, betrayed by his own kinsmen, beaten, stoned, and imprisoned. His enemies maligned his character, falsely accusing him of many evils. Yet, Paul, the prisoner of the Lord, says, 'Rejoice in the Lord', and his exhortation is enforced by his own example.

Paul knew there is marvellous power in this medicine. Most medicines are bitter, but joy in the Lord is sweet to the taste and comforting to the heart. There had been a little rift in the fellowship of two sisters in the congregation at Philippi. Euodias and Syntyche were upset with one another. I do not know what their quarrel was about. It was so petty that Paul does not even mention it. Most quarrels are just insignificant, petty gripes over insignificant, petty things. But as a cure for the disagreement between these two ladies, Paul prescribed this medicine, 'Rejoice in the Lord'. He knew that joy drives away strife and division. It is impossible to divide two hearts when both rejoice in the Lord.

If you rejoice in the Lord, you are unlikely to give offence; if you rejoice in the Lord, you are unlikely to take offence. When your heart is occupied with higher things, you are not easily disturbed by the little troubles which naturally arise among such imperfect creatures as we are. Joy in the Lord is the cure for all discord between the people of God.

After Paul admonishes us to rejoice in the Lord, he commands us to be careful for nothing, implying that the best preparation for the trials of life is to 'rejoice in the Lord alway'. Joy sustains us in the trials we face. It is a light that shines brightest when darkness is thickest. Joy in the Lord is the cure for care. Fretfulness, worry, and anxiety flee from the people of God as they rejoice in the Lord. It is exceedingly difficult for a person to be full of care who is full of joy. Being satisfied with your God, when your heart is overflowing with delight in him, when your soul is full of joy in the Lord, you will say, in the face of all your trials, 'Why art thou cast down, O my soul? and why art thou disquieted within me? hope thou in God: for I shall yet praise him, who is the health of my countenance, and my God' (Psalm 42:11). Let us who are the people of God be a thankful people. Let us 'rejoice in the Lord alway, again I say, rejoice'. All who know the Lord Jesus Christ can and should rejoice in him at all times.

Rejoice
Paul is telling us that as children of the living God it is our duty to rejoice in him. Most people imagine it really does not matter whether they rejoice or not, but it does. This is God's delightful command. It is therefore our privilege and responsibility to do it. Joy is as much a matter of obedience to God as faith and love. It is not a matter of indifference. Not only are we commanded to rejoice, but where there is true faith in the Lord Jesus Christ there is also joy in him. Joy is the fruit of the Spirit and the result of faith in Christ. It is a grace of the Spirit in the believer's heart that is seen in his life. It cannot be hidden. God's people are not a morbid, grumbling, murmuring, complaining, unhappy people. Faith in Christ produces joy in Christ (Romans 14:17; Galatians 5:22; Ephesians 5:18, 19; Philippians 3:3). Joy is a duty that

is good for us. The wise man wrote, 'A merry heart maketh a cheerful countenance: but by sorrow of the heart the spirit is broken ... A merry heart doeth good like a medicine; but a broken spirit drieth the bones' (Proverbs 15:13; 17:22).

What a gracious God we serve! He makes delight to be a duty. He makes happiness a matter of obedience. He commands us to rejoice! It will do you good and not evil to rejoice all the days of your life. Above all people in this world, the people of God should be a truly joyful people.

Many times in the Word of God we are commanded to 'rejoice in the Lord'. 'Let all those that put their trust in thee rejoice: let them even shout for joy, because thou defendest them: let them also that love thy name be joyful in thee' (Psalm 5:11). 'Be glad in the Lord, and rejoice, ye righteous: and shout for joy, all ye that are upright in heart' (Psalm 32:11). 'Let all those that seek thee rejoice and be glad in thee: let such as love thy salvation say continually, the Lord be magnified' (Psalm 40:16). 'Let the righteous be glad; let them rejoice before God: yea, let them exceedingly rejoice' (Psalm 68·3). 'Rejoice evermore' (1 Thessalonians 5:16).

This joy of which Paul speaks is a self-evident thing. It is like a candle lighted in a dark room. You do not need to sound a trumpet and say look here is light. The light proclaims itself by its own brilliance. When joy floods a person's heart, there is no need to proclaim it. It shines out of the eyes. It sparkles in the face. It flavours the speech. I know many who make a great outward show to impress others with their joy in the Lord, but their daily speech and conduct betrays anything but a joyful heart.

True joy is a very contagious thing. A truly happy, graciously happy person brings happiness and cheer to others. A believer's joy in Christ gives strength and encouragement to those who are around him. The believer's joy in Christ is a good testimony to men of the grace of God. The angels declared to the shepherds at the Saviour's birth, 'I bring you tidings of great joy' (Luke 2:10).

Our God dwells in the ineffable bliss of his own glory. He lives in the happiness of his own holy Being; and he would have us happy, too. Let the worshippers of Baal cut themselves and make hideous outcries if they will, but the servants of Jehovah must not even mar the corners of their beards. Even if they fast, they anoint their heads, wash their faces, and appear not unto men as those who fast, but as the joyful servants of the joyful God.

True joy in the Lord Jesus Christ is good for you. Joy oils the wheels of your life's machinery. Joy strengthens you for your daily labour. Joy will beautify your character. Joy will carry you through the day. Joy will give you sweet rest. We who are the people of God have every reason to rejoice (Psalm 32:1, 2).

Rejoice in the Lord

Paul shows us the source, the sphere, and the cause of the believer's joy. Someone said, 'Joy is the flag that is flown from the citadel of the heart when the King is in residence'. We do not rejoice in ourselves, in our riches, in our health, in our families, in our positions, in our talents, in our church, or in our doctrine. The source of our joy is not in or of this world. We rejoice in the Lord. He is the source of our joy. He is the sphere of our joy. He is the cause of our joy. He is the object of our joy. It is written, 'Delight thyself also in the Lord; and he shall give thee the desires of thine heart' (Psalm 37:4).

'Rejoice', children of God, 'Rejoice in the Lord'. Rejoice in the Father, your Father who is in heaven, your loving, tender, unchangeable God. Rejoice in the Son, your Redeemer, your Brother, the Husband of your soul, your Prophet, Priest, and King. Rejoice in the Holy Spirit, your Quickener, your Guide, your Comforter, who shall abide with you forever.

Particularly, I believe Paul is admonishing us to rejoice in the Lord Jesus Christ. This is a sea of joy and delight. Here are seven things about our Lord Jesus Christ which inspire joy in the believing heart.

1. Rejoice in the Lord's Person (Hebrews 1:1-3). Rejoice because he is who he is! Rejoice in his Godhead. Rejoice in his humanity, and rejoice in his attributes. Rejoice in his holiness, justice, truth, love, mercy, grace, faithfulness, immutability. If the Lord Jesus Christ is truly my joy and I rejoice in him, then I never have any reason not to rejoice, because he never changes.

2. Rejoice in the Lord's performance (Psalm 105:1, 2; 145:5). Rejoice in his covenant of mercy (Isaiah 54:10; Hosea 2:6-23). Rejoice in his perfect righteousness (Isaiah 42:21). Rejoice in his bloody sacrifice (Matthew 26:28). Rejoice in his saving grace (2 Timothy 1:9).

3. Rejoice in the Lord's position (Psalm 68:18, 19). 'God hath highly exalted him.' His is a position of power and authority. His is a position of honour and majesty. His is a position of total sovereignty.

4. Rejoice in the Lord's providence (Romans 8:28). Rejoice in the Lord's providence before your conversion, at your conversion, and after your conversion.

5. Rejoice in the Lord's provision (Psalm 13:5, 6). All our spiritual needs are provided in Christ. All our temporal needs are met by Christ. All our eternal needs are found in Christ.

6. Rejoice in the Lord's presence (Isaiah 41:10; 43:2-5). He has said, 'Where two or three are gathered together in my name, there am I in the midst of them' (Matthew 18:20).

7. Rejoice in the Lord's promise (John 14:1-3). 'The hope of the righteous shall be gladness' (Proverbs 10:28).

Rejoice in the Lord always
When the Apostle said, 'Rejoice in the Lord', he knew we would say, 'But', and then begin to make excuses for not rejoicing. Therefore, he silences all our excuses with this word 'alway'. When are we to rejoice in the Lord? 'Rejoice in the Lord alway.' 'Rejoice evermore. Pray without ceasing. In everything give thanks: for this is the will of God in Christ Jesus concerning you' (1 Thessalonians 5:16-18).

Rejoice in the Lord now. When you cannot rejoice in anything or anyone else, rejoice in the Lord (Habakkuk 3:17, 18). In days of plenty, rejoice in the Lord who gives. In days of need, rejoice in the Lord who takes away. I cannot rejoice in that which makes my eyes to weep; but I can rejoice in the Lord even when my eyes are weeping. In sorrow, rejoice in the Lord. In bereavement, rejoice in the Lord. In pain, rejoice in the Lord. In affliction, rejoice in the Lord. When your sin overwhelms you, rejoice in the Lord.

When you have other things to rejoice in, still rejoice only in the Lord. 'A man's life consisteth not in the abundance of the things which he possesseth' (Luke 12:15). If he leads you beside the still waters, restores your soul, and makes you to lie down in green pastures, remember that the Lord your Shepherd is better than all the blessings which he bestows. Rejoice not in the blessings, but in the Blesser. Rejoice not in the gift, but rejoice in the Giver.

If you have not rejoiced before, begin now. Begin at once. When you have rejoiced for a long time, keep on rejoicing in the Lord. Do not anticipate trouble, but rather rejoice in the Lord. 'Sufficient unto the day is the evil thereof' (Matthew 6:34). 'He shall not be afraid of evil tidings; his heart is fixed, trusting in the Lord' (Psalm 112:7).

When you are alone, rejoice in the Lord. When you are in the company of God's people, rejoice in the Lord. When you are in the company of the ungodly, rejoice in the Lord.

And again I say, rejoice
Do you see how Paul is urgently admonishing us? He repeats the command with emphasis upon that one word, 'Rejoice'. He says, 'Rejoice', and then he immediately emphasizes the point. It is as though he had said, 'Rejoice in the Lord alway: I said, Rejoice!' Why did he give this same commandment twice in one breath? He means for us to understand the importance of this matter and take it seriously. He exemplified this continual joy in the Lord. He rejoiced to know that he had not laboured in vain (Philippians 2:16). His farewell was a joyful farewell (Philippians 3:1). He rejoiced in the Lord when he saw the kindness and generosity of his brethren (Philippians 4:10, 18).

Paul loved the people of God at Philippi, and he truly wanted them to be happy. He knew they would face many things which would make it difficult to always rejoice. He wanted to assure them it is both possible and practical to rejoice in the Lord always. It is as though he were saying, 'Look at me. If I can rejoice in the Lord in this dungeon, surely, you can rejoice also.'

> Rejoice, believer, in the Lord,
> Who makes your cause His own.
> The hope that's built upon His Word
> Can ne'er be overthrown.
>
> Though many foes beset your road,
> And feeble is your arm,
> Your life is hid with Christ in God,
> Beyond the reach of harm.

Weak as you are, you shall not faint,
Or fainting, shall not die.
Jesus, the strength of every saint,
Will aid you from on high.

Though sometimes unperceived by sense,
Faith sees Him always near,
A guide, a glory, a defence;
Then what have you to fear?

As surely as He overcame,
And triumphed once for you,
So surely you that love His name
Shall triumph in Him too.

John Newton

Chapter 18

A Cure For Care

Rejoice in the Lord alway: and again I say, Rejoice. Let your moderation be known unto all men. The Lord is at hand. Be careful for nothing; but in every thing by prayer and supplication with thanksgiving let your requests be made known unto God. And the peace of God, which passeth all understanding, shall keep your hearts and minds through Christ Jesus ... I can do all things through Christ which strengtheneth me.

(Philippians 4:4-13)

My times are in Thy hand,
Father, I wish them there;
My life, my soul, my all I leave
Entirely to Thy care.

My times are in Thy hand
Whatever they may be,
Pleasing or painful, dark or bright,
As best may seem to Thee.

My times are in Thy hand,
Why should I doubt or fear?
A Father's hand will never cause
His child a needless tear.

My times are in Thy hand,
Jesus the Crucified!
The hand my many sins had pierced
Is now my guard and guide.

W. F. Lloyd

Do I really trust the Lord Jesus Christ? Do I really believe God? Do you? We say we believe in God's absolute sovereignty. We say 'we know that all things work together for good to them that love God, to them who are the called, according to his purpose'. We say we want the will of God to be done in all things. We even pray, 'Thy will be done, on earth as it is in heaven'. With our Lord, we have often spoken these words in prayer, 'Not my will, thy will be done. Father, glorify thy name'. All that we say and profess with our lips sounds very good. It appears very pious. But do I really believe these things? Do you?

If I really believe that the God whom I worship and trust, whose glory I seek, is absolutely, totally, and universally sovereign, why do I worry so much? If I really believe all things, both pleasant and painful, work together for my eternal good and God's eternal glory, why do I murmur when the hand of his providence sends pain, adversity, sickness, bereavement, and heartache to me? If I am really, sincerely seeking the will of God and the glory of God in all things, why do I become so distressed, despondent, and vexed when he does that which is contrary to my will?

I know the answer to those questions, and you do, too. Our worrying is a lack of faith in our God. Our murmuring and complaining is a lack of contentment with God's providence. Our despondency and distress is a lack of submission to the will of God. I say, upon the authority of Holy Scripture, that faith, real faith in the Lord Jesus Christ, is a cure for care. It is the only cure for care.

I am not talking about bravery. I am not talking about a lack of feeling or emotion. I am talking about faith, real faith in Christ. Every man makes a good soldier in a dress parade, but the real proof of a soldier is the battlefield. In the day of trial we will find out what we are made of.

Perhaps you say, 'Is it really possible for a person to display real faith, contentment, and submission in the midst of such trials as I have to face?' Abraham did (Genesis 22:14). Eli did (1 Samuel 3:18). David did (2 Samuel 12:13, 23; 23:5). Job did (Job 1:20-22; 2:9, 10). To believe God is to be joyful, submissive, peaceful, and content in Christ.

In Philippians 4, the Apostle Paul gives us plain, clear instructions about believing God. He is telling us that faith is a cure for care.

An admonition to be obeyed

In verses 4-6, Paul is saying, 'Live what you profess. Do what you say. Practise what you preach. You say, you believe God; therefore, you should live as men and women who believe God.'

First, he says, 'Rejoice in the Lord'. This word rejoice is used ten times in this epistle. We know the doctrine. We ought to rejoice in the Lord. I pray that in our hearts we may learn to rejoice, that our daily experience may be one of rejoicing in the Lord.

The admonition is, 'Rejoice in the Lord'. It is not, 'Rejoice in yourself'. It is not, 'Rejoice in what you have'. It is not, 'Rejoice in what you experience'. It is, 'Rejoice in the Lord'. Rejoice in the Lord's Person, in his presence, and in his providence.

'Rejoice in the Lord always.' Joy is never out of season, and joy is never out of reason. If I believe the Lord Jesus Christ, I should rejoice in him at all times and in all circumstances.

If I belong to Christ, being purchased by his blood and saved by his grace, I always have reason to rejoice in him. Rejoice in his grace; it is always sufficient. Rejoice in his blood; it cleanses from all sin. Rejoice in his righteousness; it justifies my soul. Rejoice in his love; it never fails. Rejoice in his intercession; it always prevails. Rejoice in his promises; they are all yea and amen. Rejoice that your names are written in heaven.

'Let your moderation be known unto all men.' The word that is here translated 'moderation' does not refer to temperance in eating and drinking, though that is certainly important. This word refers to humility and gentleness. In fact, this word is only used one other time in the New Testament. It is used in 2 Corinthians 10:1, and there it is translated the 'gentleness of Christ'.

Paul is saying, 'Let all men, both believers and unbelievers, see and recognize your humility, your unselfishness, your forgiving spirit, your thoughtfulness and consideration.' We are to deal with men, not in severity, but in gentleness and love (Ephesians 4:31, 32). We are to put up with the affronts and injuries of others, bearing them patiently and forgiving them. We are to put the best interpretation on the words and statements of others, not seeking cause for offense. We have a good reason for such a gentle spirit, 'The Lord is at hand'.

'Be careful for nothing.' Trust the Lord, and stop worrying (Matthew 10:30). Beloved, we who believe must not fret, murmur, complain, and worry about things (Psalm 37:1-8). Take your burdens, your problems, your cares to the Lord. His shoulders are broad enough and strong enough to carry your load.

Trust the Lord and give thanks. I can never come to the throne of mercy without being reminded that I have boundless mercies for which to be thankful. Why should I worry or complain?

Trust the Lord and call on him in prayer (Hebrews 4:16). All true prayer involves two things: faith and submission. I have no reason to worry about anything until God ceases to rule this world, until the blood of Christ loses its power, until the intercession of Christ has no acceptance with God, until the promise of God is broken, and until God loses his glory as God.

A promise to be believed
In verses 7 and 8, Paul tells us to rejoice in the Lord always, be gentle and caring to all men, trust the Lord. This will be the result, 'the peace of God which passeth all understanding, shall keep your hearts and minds through Christ Jesus'. Compare Isaiah 26:3.

A proper believing knowledge of the Lord Jesus Christ will give you peace. I am a man at peace, because I am at peace with God. I am a man at peace, because the great concerns of my heart are sure. God will glorify himself. The will of God shall be done. God's elect shall be saved. I am a man at peace, because God has promised to do me good, nothing but good.

Yet, we must be careful that we think upon, meditate upon, and do those things that are agreeable to peace (v. 8). 'As a man thinketh in his heart, so is he' (Proverbs 23:7). 'Keep thy heart with all diligence: for out of it are the issues of life' (Proverbs 4:23).

An example to be followed

Paul's doctrine was enforced by his deeds. His exhortations were enforced by his example. His preaching was enforced by his practice (v. 9). Paul had learned to be content (vv. 11, 12). It must be learned (Romans 5:1-5). Contentment! What a rare jewel it is (Luke 12:15; 1 Timothy 6:6-10).

Paul was content with God's purpose. He was content with God's providence. He was content with God's provision. He found his contentment in Christ (v. 13).

Here is a cure for care. Trust the Lord Jesus Christ. This is what I want for myself, and this is what I want for you who are God's children: total submission to Christ and total contentment with Christ.

> Thy way, not mine, O Lord,
> However dark it be;
> Oh lead me by Thine own right hand,
> Choose out the path for me.
>
> Smooth let it be or rough,
> It will be still the best;
> Winding or straight, it matters not,
> It leads me to Thy rest.
>
> I dare not choose my lot,
> I would not if I might;
> But choose Thou for me, O my God,
> So shall I walk aright.
>
> Take Thou my cup, and it
> With joy or sorrow fill;
> As ever best to Thee may seem,
> Choose Thou my good and ill.
>
> Choose Thou for me my friend,
> My sickness or my health;
> Choose Thou my joys and cares for me,
> My poverty or wealth.

Not mine, not mine the choice,
If things are great or small;
Be Thou my Guide, my Guard, my Strength,
My Wisdom, and my All

                    Horatius Bonar

Chapter 19

God's Way Of Peace

Be careful for nothing; but in every thing by prayer and supplication with thanksgiving let your requests be made known unto God. And the peace of God, which passeth all understanding, shall keep your hearts and minds through Christ Jesus.

(Philippians 4:6, 7)

One of the greatest ambitions a person has in this world is to live in peace. Most people live in constant turmoil, strife, and distress. Few people know anything about peace; real, lasting, continual peace. Those children who are raised in homes where mom and dad are always fussing and fighting, go to bed at night with weeping eyes and pray for peace in their home. Those men and women who are members of churches where men and women, pastor and deacons are always at odds can hardly believe it is possible for brethren to dwell together in unity. What do you suppose those mothers would give for peace who live in countries that are ravished everyday with war and terrorism? If doctors could come up with a drug that would give peace to a troubled heart and give peace to a guilty conscience, we might soon empty our institutions. I am sure that the greatest craving of the human heart is peace. Do you want peace? Do you long for peace? I want to show you God's way of peace.

I want peace with God. As a guilty sinner, by nature, my heart is at enmity against God. All men are born in rebellion to God. 'The carnal mind is enmity against God' (Romans 8:7). And because all men are guilty of sin, all men by nature are the objects of God's wrath. The only way for a guilty sinner to find peace with God is through the blood of the Lord Jesus Christ. We must be reconciled to God by the blood of Christ.

God reconciled his own elect to him by the substitutionary sacrifice of his Son in our place at Calvary (2 Corinthians 5:18-21). God reconciles his people to himself by the gracious operations of the Holy Spirit, applying the blood of Christ to our hearts by the gospel (Colossians 1:20, 21; Hebrews 9:12-14).

Peace with God comes by faith in Christ. Peace with God comes by surrender to the claims of Christ. Peace with God is in Christ (Ephesians 2:13, 14). You must begin here. This is God's way of peace. Until you bow to Christ, until you trust Christ, you will never obtain peace with God.

I want peace from God. I am a man living among men in this world. As such, I want to live in peace. I want, as much as possible, to live peaceably with all men. God, give me peace, and I have all that is needed to make me happy. This peace comes from God. Where the Prince of Peace reigns, there is peace between men. Those who know God, live in peace. Where there is strife, wrath, malice, and discord, someone does not know God (Ephesians 4:1-3). 'Behold, how good and how pleasant it is for brethren to dwell together in unity' (Psalm 133:1).

I want to enjoy the peace of God. Living in this world, in the midst of sin, sorrow, pain, and affliction, I want that peace which God gives to the hearts of his people. The most blessed thing in this world is to have a peaceful heart and a peaceful conscience.

It is both possible and profitable for those who trust Christ to enjoy the peace of God. God promises this peace to his people. It is written, 'Thou wilt keep him in perfect peace, whose mind is stayed on thee; because he trusteth in thee' (Isaiah 26:3).

This peace was purchased for God's elect by the blood of Christ. He 'made peace through the blood of his cross' (Colossians 1:20).

This blessed peace of God is the legacy of Christ, given to his people by the grace and power of the Holy Spirit. Our Lord said, 'Peace I leave with you, my peace I give unto you: not as the world giveth, give I unto you. Let not your heart be troubled, neither let it be afraid' (John 14:27). 'These things have I spoken unto you, that in me ye might have peace.

In the world ye shall have tribulation: but be of good cheer; I have overcome the world' (John 16:33). 'The fruit of the Spirit is love, joy, and peace' (Galatians 5:22).

Yet, this peace of God is something which must be appropriated by faith. This peace does not come without the exercise of faith in Christ. If we would enjoy the peace of God, we must seek it. 'Acquaint now thyself with him, and be at peace' (Job 22:21). 'Seek peace, and pursue it' (Psalm 34:14). 'Let the peace of God rule in your hearts' (Colossians 3:15). Peace comes by believing God (Matthew 11:29; Hebrews 4:3, 9, 10).

Paul tells us in Philippians 4:6, 7 how the people of God obtain the peace of God.

The problem

First, Paul attacks the problem. 'Be careful for nothing.' There is the problem. The reason we do not enjoy the peace of God is this: we are full of care about many things. Paul is not promoting irresponsibility. That would be contrary to the gospel. We all have many responsibilities which lawfully demand our care and attention in this world. But Paul is telling us not to be full of care about the things of this world. He is saying, 'Children of God, do not fret and worry. Do not have any anxious fear about anything'. If I am a believer, I have no reason to worry about anything (Psalm 23:1; John 14:1-4).

I know we all have cares that press us down, causing us to worry and fret. But, if I am a believer, none of those things which greatly disturb the peace of other men should disturb mine. Christ is my peace.

Does sin cause you to fear? Believe God (1 John 3:1-5). Do you worry about your children? Pray for them, trust God to do what is best for them, and submit them to the hand and will of God. Are you fretting because of some affliction? Submit to the hand of God's providence (Romans 8:28). Are you full of care about the mundane affairs of everyday life? Your God, who numbers the hairs on your head, will see to it your daily needs are supplied. Maybe you are perplexed about the will of God. Again, I say, trust the Lord. If you seek his will and trust him, he will direct you in doing his will (Proverbs 3:5, 6). Do you worry about the future? It is in the hands of our God. Trust him.

This is what I am saying, 'Cast all your care upon the Lord, for He careth for you' (1 Peter 5:7). Children of God, we have no business carrying the heavy load of care. Stop causing your heart so much trouble. Stop worrying. Learn to trust the Lord.

Worrying is a useless, futile endeavour. It never does any good; and it often does great harm. To worry is to make an intrusion upon God's throne. It is rebellion against his sovereign government of the world. It is a denial of his right to rule. Worry is contrary to faith. It is a lack of submission to God's providence. It dishonours our God. It dishonours the gospel.

All of our worrying reveals an undue attachment to this world. In reality, worry, fretfulness, and anxiety arise from a neglect of Christ. Have you forgotten, 'The Lord is at hand'? A real sense of Christ's presence will give you peace. The Lord God says, 'My presence shall go with thee, and I will give thee rest' (Exodus 33:14).

Children of God, 'Be careful for nothing'. When the storms of life are raging, snuggle up in the everlasting arms and be at peace. You may say, 'I try not to worry, but I just cannot stop'. Paul tells us how to stop worrying.

The solution
Paul says, 'Be careful for nothing'. Then, he tells us how to avoid anxious care. Rather than worrying, fretting, and biting your nails, 'In everything by prayer and supplication with thanksgiving let your request be made known unto God'. Your cares are many, so let your prayers be many. Turn your cares into prayers.

> What a friend we have in Jesus,
> All our sins and griefs to bear!
> What a privilege to carry
> Everything to God in prayer!
> O what peace we often forfeit,
> O what needless pain we bear,
> All because we do not carry
> Everything to God in prayer!
>
> Have we trials and temptations?
> Is there trouble anywhere?
> We should never be discouraged –
> Take it to the Lord in prayer.

Can we find a friend so faithful
Who will all our sorrows share?
Jesus knows our every weakness –
Take it to the Lord in prayer.

Are we weak and heavy laden,
Cumbered with a load of care?
Precious Saviour, still our Refuge, -
Take it to the Lord in prayer.
Do thy friends despise, forsake thee?
Take it to the Lord in Prayer;
In His arms, He'll take and shield thee –
Thou wilt find a solace there.

Joseph M. Scriven

Try to get hold of this if you can. God is interested in everything that concerns you! Paul says, 'In everything, let your requests be made known unto God'. He means everything! (Hebrews 4:16).

I am not about to describe a certain ritual for prayer, nor am I about to prescribe certain ingredients of true prayer. But I do believe there are some things which will be found in that prayer which will ease you of care. When you go to God in prayer, when you cast your care upon the Lord, be sure these seven things characterize your heart's attitude before God.

Reverence: 'After this manner therefore pray ye: Our Father which art in heaven, Hallowed be thy name' (Matthew 6:9).
Submission: 'Thy will be done in earth, as it is in heaven' (Matthew 6:10).
Honesty: 'Let your requests be made known unto God' (Philippians 4:6).
Selflessness: 'Ye ask, and receive not, because ye ask amiss, that ye may consume it upon your lusts' (James 4:3).
Importunity: 'Ask, and it shall be given you; seek and ye shall find; knock, and it shall be opened unto you, For every one that asketh

receiveth; and he that seeketh findeth; and to him that knocketh it shall be opened' (Luke 11:9, 10).

Faith: Faith in the blood of Christ, in the righteousness of Christ, in the goodness of God, in the power of God, and in the promise of God. 'And all things, whatsoever ye shall ask in prayer, believing, ye shall receive' (Matthew 21:22).

Thanksgiving: 'Giving thanks always for all things unto God and the Father in the name of our Lord Jesus Christ' (Ephesians 5:20).

God hears and honours and answers such prayer. He may delay the request, but he will not deny it. He may deny the earthly good, but he will give a far richer heavenly good.

The blessed results

'And the peace of God, which passeth all understanding, shall keep your hearts and minds through Christ Jesus.' If you will cast your care upon the Lord, if you will call upon him in persevering, believing prayer, you shall have the peace of God.

This peace comes from God. Only the God of peace can give you peace. A man can never live in peace until he comes to know God. A woman can never live in peace until she comes to know God. And the more we know of God, the more peaceful our heart within will be.

This peace is an unfathomable, immeasurable, inexplicable peace. It is the peace of God. Spurgeon said, it is 'the unruffled serenity of the infinitely happy God, the eternal composure of the absolutely contented God'. Other people will not understand it. You will not be able to explain it. You cannot understand it yourself.

Our Lord says to the raging storm, 'Be still', and all is at peace. This blessed peace is a guardian over the hearts and minds of God's elect. This peace comes to men through the Lord Jesus Christ. What he said to his troubled disciples before his crucifixion, he says to us also, 'Let not your heart be troubled: ye believe in God, believe also in me. In my Father's house are many mansions: if it were not so, I would have told you, I go to prepare a place for you. And if I go and prepare a place for you, I will come again, and receive you unto myself; that where I am, there ye may be also' (John 14:1-3).

The story is told of a martyr imprisoned for his faith in the Lord Jesus Christ. The night before he was to be beheaded, he was able to sleep so soundly, so peacefully that the prison guard had to come in the prison cell and shake him to awaken him the morning of his execution. May God give each of us such peace!

Chapter 20

The Rare Jewel Of Christian Contentment

Not that I speak in respect of want: for I have learned, in whatsoever state I am, therewith to be content.

(Philippians 4:11)

Paul tells us something in our text that few men can honestly affirm. He says, 'I have learned, in whatsoever state I am, therewith to be content'. This contentment of which Paul speaks is something which must be learned. It is not a virtue men possess by nature and it is something which very few who live in this world ever learn. The vast majority of professing Christians have absolutely no knowledge of the peace of God. I have personally seen men ruin their ministry simply because they were not content with what God was doing, or were not content with their station in life. Many people simply cannot function in day by day life situations because they have no contentment. Yet, nothing more beautifully adorns the gospel of the grace of God, which we profess to believe, than this blessed jewel of contentment.

Contentment is the satisfaction of the believing heart with God's good providence. It is a willing, peaceful submission and resignation of the heart to the will of God. Contentment is a satisfaction with things as they are, realizing that all things are as God would have them. Charles Buck described contentment like this, 'Contentment is a disposition of mind in which our desires are confined to what we enjoy, without murmuring at our lot, or wishing ardently for more.' And Jeremiah Burroughs said, 'Christians contentment is that sweet, inward, quiet, gracious frame of spirit, which freely submits to, and delights in God's wise and Fatherly disposal in every condition.'

Be sure you understand what I am saying. I am not saying we should have no interest in our own welfare, or in the welfare of our families. I am not saying we should be idle, negligent, and irresponsible. I am not saying we should not be diligent in the pursuit of our worldly careers. These things would be contrary to the Word of God. The believer should be the most diligent, most responsible, most reliable, and most resourceful man or woman in the world. But I am saying that our cares in this world must be moderated and governed by our confidence in our God. The believer does not find contentment in his condition in life. He finds contentment in Christ who is our life.

This contentment of heart, this inward, peaceful satisfaction with Christ, is altogether contrary to the natural tendencies and disposition of our hearts. We are all terribly proud creatures. We have nothing to be proud of, but we are so proud. For the most part, it is our pride that keeps us from being content. Pride says, 'I deserve better'. Pride murmurs and complains.

Proud men are naturally envious men (Psalm 73:3). Proud men are naturally covetous men. Man is like the horseleech, crying, 'Give, give, more, more'. Covetousness is idolatry; it is an anxious, immoderate desire for more than you possess (Proverbs 30:15, 16). Proud men are naturally ambitious men. A proud man cannot endure the thought of something being above him and superior to him. I have read that Alexander the Great, who was considered one of history's most successful military commanders, after he had conquered all the nations around him and built one of the largest empires in the ancient world, sat down and wept, because there were no more nations to conquer. How sad, and how much like him we are.

These are the things that are natural to the fallen sons of Adam. But Paul declares, 'I have learned, in whatsoever state I am, therewith to be content'. Then he gives us a commentary on his words. He says this is what I mean, 'I know both how to be abased, and I know how to abound: everywhere and in all things I am instructed both to be full and to be hungry, both to abound and to suffer need.'

The Lord our God would have his people to be a content people (1 Timothy 6:6-8; Hebrews 13:5). John Newton wrote,

Content with beholding His face
My all to His pleasure resigned,
No changes of season or place
Would make any change in my mind.
While blest with a sense of His love,
A palace a toy would appear,
And prisons would palaces prove,
If Jesus would dwell with me there.

Why be content?

Why should we be satisfied with our lot, state, and condition in life? Why should we avoid all of our natural, sinful tendencies to worry, fret, murmur, and complain? Why live without envy, covetousness, and ambition? Why should we be content? For the glory of God.

We should be content, always and in all things, for the glory of our God and Saviour. Let us never give the enemies of our God reason to blaspheme. Everything you do has an impression upon those who are around you. But above all things, your attitude tells men what you really believe about God. We have a strong God upon whom we can lean, no matter how bad our circumstances.

We should be content for the gospel's sake. For the honour of the gospel we profess to believe we ought to show a disposition which reflects the gospel. One who is always upset and complaining about something does not honour the gospel they profess.

We should be content for the comfort and encouragement of our brethren. Contentment is contagious. Strength encourages strength.

We who believe should be content before our God because all that we know and experience tells us we ought to be content with our present possessions, our present circumstances, our present position, our present responsibilities, our present advantages, and our present afflictions.

We all have and enjoy in this world much better than we deserve. We all have reason to say with Jacob, 'I am not worthy of the least of all thy mercies' (Genesis 32:10). 'It is of the Lord's mercies that we are not consumed, because his compassions fail not' (Lamentations 3:22). We know all things in this world are but temporary. The good that

157

brightens our day is temporary. The bad that darkens our way is temporary.

Presently we enjoy the very best possible good (Romans 8:32). John Gill said, 'The people of God have all things in hand, or in promise, or in sure and certain hope'. Surely, all who know God may say with Jacob, 'I have enough'. God has given us all things richly to enjoy. All things pertaining to life and godliness, all things pertaining to grace and glory are ours. What more could be desired?

I have all I need. I have all that it is best for me to have. I have all that I have the ability to wisely use for the glory of God, the gospel of God, and the good of my fellow man. Therefore, I have enough. I am content.

The eternal God is my God. God the Father is my covenant God. God the Son is my Surety. God the Spirit is my Comforter. All the blessings of God in the covenant of grace are mine (Ephesians 1:3-14). Redemption, righteousness, pardon, justification, acceptance, eternal glory are all mine in Christ.

God has favoured me with his most precious earthly gifts. He has given me the gospel, the ordinances, the fellowship of his saints, and has called me to the work of the ministry. The Lord God has blessed me with the best of all temporal provisions. He has given me a happy home, a healthy body, and a comfortable life. I say there is no reason for any of us who are born of God not to be content.

How to learn contentment?

I realize this contentment does not come naturally to men. Paul said he had 'learned to be content'. How does the believer learn contentment? Here are three things which teach the believer to be content.

First, the grace of God that brings salvation teaches us to be content. Contentment is a gift and work of divine grace. The knowledge of God teaches us we ought to be content and plants within us a desire for contentment.

Second, the believer's experience in this world, in the providence of God, instructs him in the way of contentment (Romans 5:1-5; Hebrews 12:5-11).

Third, faith in Christ teaches us to be content. The more we grow in faith, in the grace and knowledge of our Lord Jesus Christ, the more we grow in contentment. The more we know Christ, the more precious he becomes. The more we trust Christ, the more confident our faith becomes. The more precious Christ is, and the more fully we trust him, the more content we are with him. In the words of the hymnwriter, 'The things of earth grow strangely dim, in the light of his glory and grace'.

What is the basis for contentment?
It is not enough for us simply to know that we should be content. It is not enough for us to say contentment is a good, desirable thing. If we would find true contentment for our hearts, we must have some foundation upon which we may confidently rest.

I rest my soul, finding real contentment at all times and in all things, on the purpose of God. I know all things are done according to God's sovereign, eternal purpose of predestination. I know God's purpose of predestination is for the eternal good of his elect (Romans 11:36). I rest my soul upon the providence of God (Romans 8:28; Psalm 97:1, 2). I rest my soul upon the power of God, the presence of God, and the promises of God.

Open the Book of God's promises. They are, to all who are in Christ Jesus, certain and sure, yea and amen. This is a blessed source of contentment. The promises of God are exceedingly great and precious. He promises to guide in the way I should go. He promises with every temptation to make a way of escape (1 Corinthians 10:13). He promises grace sufficient to meet every need (2 Corinthians 12:9). He promises a good end to all my troubles. He promises strength for every work. He promises help for every time of need (Hebrews 4:16). He promises that he will soon come for his own (John 14:1-3), and a life of eternal satisfaction with him. Newton again says,

> The Lord has promised good to me,
> His Word my hope secures:
> He will my strength and portion be,
> As long as life endures.
> And when this heart and flesh shall fail,
> And mortal life shall cease,
> I shall possess within the vail
> A life of joy and peace.

When should we be content?
Let us be content always. Let us be content in all things; in poverty and in wealth, in sickness and in health, in joy and in sorrow, in success and in adversity. Let us be content in all places; in our work, in our home, in our place in God's church, in the work God has given us to do for the honour of his name.

What are the results of contentment?
Contentment of heart will give strength, courage, and boldness. Contentment will give you a mind free of care. It will give you peace. Contentment is like an anchor for the soul. It holds a little vessel steady, even in the raging storms of life. Horatio Spafford says,

> When peace, like a river, attendeth my way,
> When sorrows like sea billows roll –
> Whatever my lot, Thou has taught me to say,
> It is well, it is well with my soul.

> Though Satan should buffet, though trials should come,
> Let this blest assurance control,
> That Christ hath regarded my helpless estate,
> And hath shed His own blood for my soul.

Chapter 21

What Can I Do?

I can do all things through Christ which strengtheneth me.

Philippians 4:13

Frequently, I have men and women suggest to me that as a preacher I should give people something to do. They would have me to preach certain things for people to do and certain things for people not to do. They would have us to preach more of what they call 'practical godliness'. They want us to lay down laws and rules and regulations to govern the lives of God's people. Of course, as with all systems of works religion, they would have us to promise certain rewards for varying degrees of obedience and threaten certain forms of punishment for varying degrees of disobedience. Law must always be enforced with rewards and punishments. Otherwise, it will be ignored.

All the heresies which have arisen throughout the history of the Christian church have two things in common, all heresies have a decided tendency to dishonour God and exalt man. All heresy makes God less than he is and makes man more than he is. Heresy has for its goal the dethronement of God and the exaltation of man. By robbing God of his sovereignty and the glory due unto his name, all prophets of deceit would cast a counterfeit lustre upon the head of rebellious and depraved creatures. All heretics will, to a greater or lesser degree, deny the sovereignty of Divine grace and give dignity to the works of man. C. H. Spurgeon wrote concerning this, 'On the other hand, the doctrines of the gospel, commonly known as the doctrines of grace, are

161

distinguished for this peculiarity above every other, namely that they sink the creature very low, and present the Lord Jehovah before us sitting upon a throne, high and lifted up.'

This fact is so true and evident that it may always distinguish truth from error. You may not be able to refute the doctrines of men, but you can be sure of this, anything that exalts man and robs God of his total, glorious sovereignty is heresy. The youngest babe in Christ may infallibly determine the truthfulness or the falsehood of any doctrine by the simple test, does it glorify God? If it does, it is true. Believe it and rejoice in it. Does it exalt man? If it does, it is false. Reject and despise it. It must not be tolerated. If, on the other hand, the doctrine lays man very low, and speaks of him in terms that makes him feel his degradation, you may be sure it is full of truth. If it puts the crown on the head of the eternal God, and not upon the head of man's freewill or good works, then it is assuredly the doctrine of Holy Scripture. It is the very truth of God.

I want to answer this question, 'What can I do?' In doing so, I want to do what I can to honour and exalt the Lord Jesus Christ, our God and Saviour; and I want to do what I can to destroy the high hopes and proud looks of self-righteous, self-applauding, sinful flesh.

Our Lord Jesus Christ answers the question
In John 15:5, our Saviour says, 'Without me ye can do nothing'. The sooner we learn this, the better. In and of ourselves, we cannot do anything, except sin. Take our Lord's statement to the widest possible extent of human existence and activity, and it still stands true – 'Without me ye can do nothing'.

The text does not say, 'Without me ye can hardly do anything,' as if to imply that with much determination and struggling, with great effort of mind and will and body, there are some things which man can do. It says, 'Without me ye can do nothing', absolutely, positively nothing at all.

The text does not say, 'Without me you cannot do some great things', as if to imply there are some small things you can do on your own. Get this right! You are dependent upon the power of God to perform the lowest, smallest acts of life; and you are certainly dependent upon God to perform the smallest, most insignificant acts of spiritual life.

John Newton said, 'The grace of God is as necessary to create a right temper in Christians on the breaking of a china plate as on the death of an only son.'

Nor does the text say, 'Without me ye cannot do anything perfectly'. It says, 'Without me ye can do nothing'.

The text does not say, 'Without me ye can begin nothing', as if to imply that there are some things which must be begun by God which are dependent upon man for completion. The text says, 'Without me ye can do nothing'.

There is not a single thing a man or a woman can do in and of themselves. We are all utterly without strength and helpless. One of the old writers was exactly right when he said, 'I am nothing. I have nothing. I can do nothing. And if I come to nothing, nothing will be lost'.

Our Lord was speaking to his disciples, those who trusted him and followed him, when he said, 'Without me ye can do nothing'. He was not talking to men and women who were lost, blind, and dead spiritually. He was talking to people like us, people to whom he had given life and faith. He was talking to regenerate, believing men and women who were his devoted followers, and he said to them, 'Without me ye can do nothing'.

These are the words of our Lord to you and me. 'Without me ye can do nothing!' Without Christ we can do nothing that pleases God. God is not pleased with what you do. God is not pleased with what I do. God is only pleased with what his Son does. We are 'accepted in the Beloved' (Ephesians 1:6).

We can perform no duty, fulfil no responsibility, carry on no work, and engage in no activity which God will accept apart from Christ. Our very best deeds of righteousness are filthy rags in God's sight. Our very best deeds must be washed in the blood of Christ and sanctified by his righteousness, or God will never accept them.

Without Christ you will never offer God a gift or a prayer that he will accept (1 Peter 2:5). Do you really think your prayers are worthy of God's acceptance? Do you think your devotions are worthy of God's approval? Do you imagine your gifts are worthy of God's gratitude? Do you suppose your works are worthy of God's reward?

Without Christ you cannot endure the slightest trial or resist the slightest temptation. With Christ Peter can walk upon the water;

without Christ he began to sink. With Christ Peter can defy a band of trained soldiers; without Christ he trembles before a little maid. With Christ Job can endure the loss of all things; without Christ he crumbles before the scathing words of men. With Christ Jonah is a bold prophet; without Christ he is enraged by a gourd. With Christ Abraham offers his son to God; without Christ he offers his wife to a heathen king.

Without Christ you cannot persevere in the faith for another moment (Philippians 1:6; 1 Peter 1:4, 5; John 10:28, 29). We know that the whole of our salvation, from start to finish, depends upon Christ and Christ alone. We have learned, by painful experience, that our Lord's statement is true 'Without me ye can do nothing'. Do you ask, 'What can I do?' In and of yourself you can do absolutely nothing! He alone preserves us, holds us, and keeps us.

Children of God, do not depend upon yourselves. You have nothing to be proud of. Of all men we ought to be the most humble and self-abasing creatures on God's earth (1 Corinthians 4:7). Do not ever forget this word of our Lord, 'Without me ye can do nothing'. Newton again,

> Once I thought my mountain strong,
> Firmly fixed, no more to move:
> Then my Saviour was my song,
> Then my soul was filled with love;
> Those were happy, golden days,
> Sweetly spent in prayer and praise.
>
> Little then myself I knew,
> Little thought of Satan's power;
> Now I feel my sins anew –
> Now I feel the stormy hour!
> Sin has put my joys to flight,
> Sin has turned my day to night.
>
> Saviour shine and cheer my soul,
> Bid my dying hopes revive;
> Make my wounded spirit whole,
> Far away the tempter drive:
> Speak the word and set me free,
> Let me live alone to Thee!

If this is true with regard to God's own people, it is equally true of every unbeliever. We do not tell sinners what they should do or what they can do to be saved for one simple reason, 'You can do nothing'. Spiritually, you are dead. The fact that you are dead in sin precludes all possibility of your doing anything (Ephesians 2:1-3). You cannot redeem your soul. You cannot atone for your sin. You cannot give yourself life. You cannot perform righteousness. You cannot renew your heart. You cannot change your nature. You cannot do anything good in the sight of God. You cannot repent of your sins. You cannot give yourself faith in Christ. You cannot come to Christ.

Your only hope is that the Lord Jesus Christ will come to you and do for you what you cannot do for yourself. He says, 'Without me ye can do nothing'.

And, my friends, without Christ there is nothing you and I can do for sinners. The church today needs to have this fact driven right into her heart. Preachers, evangelists, teachers, missionaries, you are powerless. You have no strength. You have no ability. You cannot do a single thing for the conversion of sinners without the power of God the Holy Spirit. It is yet true, 'Without me ye can do nothing'.

'Our sufficiency is of God' (2 Corinthians 2:14-17; 3:5). If we ever truly realize this fact, we will become men and women of earnest, intense prayer. What can I do? Our Lord answers the question for us. 'Without me ye can do nothing.' Be sure you learn it and never forget it. Without Christ you can do nothing. Does that thought fill you with despair? It should not. Despair, rather, of all self-sufficiency. That is good. I am sufficient for nothing in myself but sin. So, then, what can I do?

The Apostle Paul answers the question
Paul says, 'I can do all things through Christ which strengtheneth me'. He speaks not of self-sufficiency. That is destroyed. We have no self-sufficiency. But we who believe do have a Christ-sufficiency, and that is all-sufficiency. Looking at the guard standing over him and the iron chains on his hands and feet, realizing he would soon face the executioner, Paul turned his eyes of faith up toward his God and Saviour, and boldly declared, 'I can do all things through Christ which strengtheneth me'.

Paul, what do you mean by such a statement? Paul felt he was qualified to do whatever God might call him to do, knowing that what God called him to do, he would enable him to do.

And I can, by the grace and presence and strength of Christ, perform whatever duties my God calls me to perform. I can, by the grace of God, patiently endure any trial which God is pleased to lay upon me (1 Corinthians 10:13). My trials come from my God and are for my good. My trials are for the good of my brethren and for the glory of God. God himself shall go with me through my trials. He will hold me by the right hand of his righteousness and sustain me.

I can, by the grace of God, overcome all the enemies of my soul (1 John 4:4). I am no longer the servant of sin. I am dead to this world. Satan is a defeated foe. We are more than conquerors through him that loved us and gave himself for us. 'And the God of peace shall bruise Satan under your feet shortly' (Romans 16:20).

I have no doubt that Paul meant for us to understand that he was saying, 'I can serve and honour my God in every state and condition I experience through Christ who strengthens me' (Philippians 4:11, 12); in poverty, in wealth, in sickness, in health, in youth, in old age, in life and in death.

What was true of Paul is true of all believers. We can do all things through Christ which strengthens us. His grace is sufficient; and having his grace, I am sufficient in him (2 Corinthians 12:9). His grace is sufficient to strengthen me for every day's labour, to support me in every trial, to hold me in every temptation, to restore me from every fall, to preserve me unto the end, and to present me holy, unblameable, and unreproveable before the presence of his glory.

Christ is my Sufficiency, and his sufficiency is all-sufficiency. His righteousness is sufficient to make me accepted. His blood is sufficient to cleanse me. His grace is sufficient to save me. His strength is sufficient to preserve me. He is sufficient to satisfy me.

What can you do? Without Christ you can do nothing. Through Christ you can do all things. Trust Christ for all things. Set your heart to do all that God bids you do, and do it through the grace and strength of Christ, for the honour and glory of his name.

Chapter 22

The Church And Her Ministers

Those things, which ye have both learned, and received, and heard, and seen in me, do: and the God of peace shall be with you ... The grace of our Lord Jesus Christ be with you all.

(Philippians 4:9-23)

This final portion of Paul's letter to the Philippians reveals much about the relationship which existed between Paul, Epaphroditus, and the church at Philippi. Paul was the faithful Apostle, the missionary who went from place to place preaching the gospel and establishing churches. Though he did not live at Philippi, and though they seldom saw his face, Paul was as much a part of the church family at Philippi as any other member of the congregation. Their hearts were joined to one another in love. The church at Philippi highly esteemed Paul for his work in the gospel. They thought of him often, spoke to one another about his work, prayed for him, encouraged him, and supported him financially.

Epaphroditus was the loving, faithful pastor of the congregation. We do not know much about Epaphroditus, but it is clear he was a gentle, loving, and faithful pastor (Philippians 2:25-30). There was no jealousy or competition between Paul and Epaphroditus. They loved one another, helped one another, comforted one another, and encouraged one another in the work of the gospel. Epaphroditus knew he was in the place God had put him in the body of Christ. He was not Paul. He was not an apostle. But he was in the place where he was most needed and most useful, and he faithfully served God in that place. He was gifted for the work the Lord had for him to do, and he faithfully gave himself to that work.

Paul knew he, too, was in the place God had put him in the body of Christ. He was in the place for which he was most gifted and where he was most useful, and he faithfully served the Lord in that place.

Paul and Epaphroditus were fellowsoldiers, brothers, companions in the work of the gospel. Both men loved Christ. Both preached the gospel and sought the glory of Christ. Both did the will of God. Both laboured for the good of the church and sought the salvation of God's elect. Both were used of God. The church at Philippi loved, supported, prayed for, and obeyed both Paul and Epaphroditus.

In Philippians 4:9-23, Paul is encouraging the church at Philippi with regard to the work of the ministry and congratulating them for their support of those who preach the gospel. Basically, Paul tells the church at Philippi three things in these verses:

He tells them to follow his example (v. 10)
He tells them not to be overly concerned about his condition (vv. 10-13). Paul did not want them to fret and worry about him. He knew he was in the place of God's choosing and God's care for him had not been suspended. He rejoiced in the church's loving care for him (v. 10). He wanted them to know he was content with his lot and condition for the gospel's sake (vv. 11-13). He assured them of his confidence that whatever the Lord called him to do, he would give him also strength to do it (v. 13).

Paul tells the saints at Philippi that they had done well in their gifts and sacrifices to him (vv. 14-19). They had supported him when he went to preach in Macedonia and Thessalonica. They supported him while he was in prison at Rome. Paul assured them that so long as they desired to support him, God would give them the ability to do so (v. 19). In all things, Paul wanted nothing but the glory of God and the spiritual, eternal welfare of God's people (vv. 20-23).

Every true preacher of the gospel and every true local church should reflect the spirit and attitude of Paul and Epaphroditus and this church. We see in Paul, Epaphroditus, and the church at Philippi an example of the responsibilities of preachers and churches to one another.

True gospel preachers are gifts of Christ to his church
God, in his infinite mercy and wisdom, has ordained the use of certain means to accomplish his purpose. The means which God has ordained for the salvation of his elect and the edification of his church is the preaching of the gospel (Romans 10:17; 1 Corinthians 1:21).

Whenever God speaks to a man, he does it by a man. If God intends to save a man, he will send a man to preach to him. If God intends to teach a man, he will send a man to preach the gospel to him. God always speaks to men by a man.

The Ethiopian could not understand the Scriptures until Philip came and preached Christ to him. Cornelius could not believe on Christ until Peter came and preached Christ to him. Lydia's heart could never be opened until she heard Paul preach the gospel. Mark it down, if God ever speaks to you, it will be by the voice of a preacher.

The greatest gift God can ever bestow upon a church, a community, or any group of people is to send them a faithful gospel preacher, and the greatest curse God can ever bring upon a people is to silence the voice of his servant among them.

Gospel preachers are God's gift to the world. 'And he gave some, apostles; and some, prophets; and some, evangelists; and some, pastors and teachers' (Ephesians 4:11).

Apostles were not limited to any particular church, but had the care of all the churches. These were the inspired penmen of the New Testament. There are no apostles today.

Prophets are men who have extraordinary gifts for explaining the Word of God. Prophets are men through whom God speaks with extraordinary power.

Evangelists are men who travel from place to place preaching the gospel, establishing churches, and strengthening the saints of God. They are itinerate preachers and missionaries, such as Philip and Barnabas.

Pastors and Teachers: Pastor-Teacher is one office in the church of Christ. The pastor is the teacher, the overseer, the bishop, the spiritual ruler of the church. He is the shepherd under Christ, who cares for the flock, feeds it, and protects it.

Christ places men in his church as he sees fit. He gives them the gifts and qualifications for the work of the gospel. Let no man presume to take the work of the ministry upon himself. God determines where his servants labour, how they labour, when they labour, and the success of their labours.

Our Lord has given his church men to preach the gospel to her for her own welfare. 'For the perfecting of the saints, for the work of the ministry, for the edifying of the body of Christ' (Ephesians 4:12).

Men called of God have great responsibilities placed upon them

Much could and should be said about a preacher's responsibilities to the church and to God. Paul explained to young Timothy what the work of the ministry involves in 1 Timothy 4:12-16 and again in 2 Timothy 4:1-5.

Basically, the preacher has three responsibilities. He must feed the church of God with the gospel, with knowledge and understanding. He must protect the church from all false teaching and from any that would turn them away from the simplicity that is in Christ. And he must labour for the increase of the church, ever seeking the Lord's sheep.

Every true gospel preacher must and will give himself wholeheartedly to the work of the ministry. The work of the ministry requires all of a man, all of his time, all of his care, all of his labour. He must give himself entirely to the work. God requires faithfulness in study, in prayer, in meditation, and in preaching.

Because the pastor is responsible for the congregation, he must rule the congregation. The pastor's oversight and rule of God's church is not one of harsh domination. It is a loving, gentle, but firm oversight. Pastors are to rule the church of Christ just as husbands are to rule their homes. They are to rule the church for the glory of Christ, for the furtherance of the gospel, for the good of the church, and for the increase of the church by the salvation of sinners. The voice of authority in God's church is the Word of God.

The church's responsibilities to her ministers

We recognize that preachers are nothing in themselves. It is true, 'The preacher is just a man'. Yet, if he is a true servant of Christ, as we have seen, he is God's man; he must be treated as such. 'Let a man so account of us, as of the ministers of Christ, and stewards of the mysteries of God' (1 Corinthians 4:1).

We who believe are to love, honour, and highly esteem the servants of God, receiving them as the Lord's servants. 'We beseech you, brethren, to know them which labour among you, and are over you in the Lord, and admonish you; And to esteem them very highly in love for their work's sake. And be at peace among yourselves' (1 Thessalonians 5:12, 13). When he sent Epaphroditus to them, Paul told the church at Philippi to 'receive him therefore in the Lord with all gladness; and hold such in reputation' (Philippians 2:29).

Believers are to submit themselves to those men who the Lord places over them. 'Remember them which have the rule over you, who have spoken unto you the word of God: whose faith follow, considering the end of their conversation' (Hebrews 13:7). 'Obey them that have the rule over you, and submit yourselves: for they watch for your souls, as they that must give account, that they may do it with joy, and not with grief: for that is unprofitable for you' (Hebrews 13:17).

Remember those men who faithfully preach the gospel. Remember their example. Remember their doctrine. Follow their faith and obey them. In all matters, doctrinal and spiritual, the servants of God who preach unto you the Word of God are to be obeyed. You are responsible to search the Scriptures and know whether the preacher is preaching the Word of God. If he is, you must obey, willingly.

Pray for your pastor and for those men God has raised up to preach the gospel (Colossians 4:3; 2 Thessalonians 3:1). Pray for your pastor with respect to his private studies and preparation as he seeks God's message for your souls. Pray for him when he stands to preach the Word. Pray for him that he will be kept, and that he will honour God in his life and conduct in this world.

Those who faithfully preach the gospel are to be supported and maintained in their livelihood by the churches of Christ. 'Let the elders that rule well be counted worthy of double honour, especially they who labour in the word and doctrine. For the scripture saith, Thou shalt not muzzle the ox that treadeth out the corn. And, the labourer is worthy of his reward' (1 Timothy 5:17, 18).

Chapter 23

The Lord Will Provide

But my God shall supply all your need according to his riches in glory by Christ Jesus.

(Philippians 4:19)

Paul the aged was in prison at Rome. Most likely he would soon be put to death, yet he was calm, quiet, peaceful, and even full of great joy. Paul's heart had been touched by the kindness and generosity of the church at Philippi.

The saints at Philippi were not wealthy people, but they were full of love and generosity. They took up a collection and sent it to Paul by their beloved pastor, Epaphroditus. It was a gift inspired by love, given in the name of God, made for the glory of God, to supply the needs of the servant of God. The little church at Philippi thought not of their own needs, but of the man of God who had preached the gospel to them, and was now suffering for the gospel's sake. They would not abandon him. Out of their slender means, they determined to do what they could for God's servant.

This church at Philippi loved Christ, loved his people, loved his gospel, and loved his servants who faithfully preached the gospel of his grace. Again and again, they generously ministered to Paul's necessity. Lydia was not about to forget that man who had shown her the way of life. The Philippian jailor would not neglect that man who had brought him the good news of freedom in Christ. The church at Philippi would never forsake that man who had taught them the gospel.

I can almost picture Paul in that dungeon. A gleam of sunlight seems to light up his cell. He is happy. His heart begins to dance. His eyes glisten with joy. He imagined he had been forgotten by all, that none stood with him, save his Lord. But now, in his deep poverty, affliction, and desertion, he had been kindly remembered by the people of God in Philippi. Just when he was most distressed, the saints at Philippi came to his aid with a gift of love; and he was charmed with the love which sent the gift to him.

We do not know what the gift was. Perhaps it was a coat, some books, some copies of the Scriptures, maybe a few gifts prepared by the members of the church, and a little money. At any rate, if measured by the standards of men, I feel sure the gift was not of very great value. But it was of great value to Paul. As David highly valued that refreshing water which his three valiant men hazarded their lives to get for him, Paul cherished the Philippians' gift.

Yet, there was nothing selfish about Paul's joy. He did not speak in respect of want. He knew how to suffer need without complaint. He looked upon this kind contribution as a fruit of the grace of God in the Philippians, a generous proof they had been lifted out of natural human selfishness into Christian love by Divine grace.

After giving thanks to God, Paul carefully expressed his deep gratitude to those who had given so graciously, generously, and freely to him. He sits down and writes this letter of thanks to his brethren at Philippi. He says to his dear friends, 'I have all, and abound, I am full, having received of Epaphroditus the things which were sent from you, an odour of a sweet smell, a sacrifice acceptable, well-pleasing to God'. His heart was evidently touched, as he pens the words, 'I rejoiced in the Lord greatly that your care of me hath flourished again'. Their little gift had done much good.

A great promise
Paul said to the saints at Philippi, 'You have sent Epaphroditus to me with your gift. You have helped me out of your deep poverty'. Then he made this promise to them, 'My God shall supply all your need'. He is able to supply all daily needs. He is able to supply all great needs and all small needs. He is able to supply all needs in all circumstances (Psalm 23:1; 34:10; 37:23-25; Matthew 6:25-34).

This promise was made to the saints at Philippi. But it was made by inspiration of God the Holy Spirit and is preserved in the Word of God as a promise most assuredly given to all who are numbered among God's elect. This is not a blanket promise given to all men. It is a promise given to the children of God; men and women of faith. As we faithfully serve him with what we have, the Lord our God will supply all our need.

The grace of God teaches the children of God to be kind and generous. The preacher of the gospel should never put his hearers under the legal bondage of tithing, or put them under the bondage of making pledges. He should not threaten them with punishment, nor bribe them with promise of reward. Giving must be motivated by the love of Christ. Let the love of Christ measure out your gifts. If motivated by the love of Christ, I can make this solemn promise from the Word of God, 'My God shall supply all your need according to his riches in glory by Christ Jesus'.

A great necessity

What a needy people we are. We have temporal, personal, and spiritual needs. For sin, we need pardon (1 John 1:9). For service, we need strength (2 Corinthians 12:9). When suffering, we need grace (2 Corinthians 12:9). The poor need to be kept from covetousness. The lonely need companionship. The sorrowing need comfort. The influential need to be kept from pride. The leaders need wisdom. The weak need help. The dying need hope. The tempted need preserving. The fallen need restoring. We need to be quickened by the Word of God, illuminated by the Spirit of God, instructed in the truth of God, kept by the grace of God, and cleansed by the blood of God's own dear Son.

Child of God, our needs are great, but do not despair. God is able to supply all temporal needs, all personal needs, and all spiritual needs. He is able to:

Pardon every sin (1 John 1:9; 2:1, 2).
Supply grace for every trial and temptation (1 Corinthians 10:13).
Strengthen for every labour (1 Thessalonians 5:24).
Recover from every fall (Psalm 37:24; Proverbs 24:16).
Deliver from every affliction (Psalm 34:19).

Comfort every sorrow (John 14:18).
Instruct in the gospel (Ephesians 4:11-14).
Direct in the will of God (Proverbs 3:5, 6).
Preserve in grace (John 10:28, 29).
Give his Divine presence (Hebrews 13:5).

It is true, our needs are great and may increase every day, but the promise still stands. 'My God shall supply all your needs according to his riches in glory by Christ Jesus.'

A great principle

God's saints are not mercenaries. We do not give to get. If you give to get gain, your giving is selfish and sinful, an abomination to God. But if you give, out of a heart of love for Christ, and give generously to the work of the gospel, God will honour your gifts by entrusting more to your care. This is a fact that cannot be disputed. Those who honour God are honoured by God. God says, 'Them that honour me I will honour' (1 Samuel 2:30). This is the principle constantly illustrated throughout the Word of God (Proverbs 3:9, 10; Malachi 3:10-12; Luke 6:38; 2 Corinthians 9:5-8).

Let us ever remember that all we possess, we possess as stewards under God. Nothing we have is for our own private consumption or use, but is given to us by God and is to be used for his glory.

This is the principal Paul sets forth when he told the Philippians, 'You have been generous in helping the Lord's servant, and the Lord will see to it that you do not suffer for doing so. Up to the measure of your ability you have served his church and helped to carry on his work in the world, and God will, therefore, supply your need.'

It is a proven fact that those who use well what God has given them will have more to use well. Your generosity does not merit God's favour in any way. But your generosity, or lack of it, reveals what you are.

The Great Provider

To supply our enormous and multiplied needs, our text sets before us a Great Provider. 'My God!' Whose God is that? Paul's God! And Paul's God is my God. If you are born of his Spirit, if you trust his dear Son, he is your God, too. Here is one area in which the greatest saint in heaven and the weakest saint on earth are completely equal. Paul's God is my God. Paul's God is your God. My brother, my sister, Paul's God is your God.

Who is this God? Paul tells us that he is the creator of all things (Hebrews 1:10), the sustainer of all things (Hebrews 1:3), the owner of all things (1 Corinthians 8:6), and the ruler of all things (2 Corinthians 5:18). 'My God' is everywhere present and everywhere omnipotent. He can supply all your need all the time. God can supply all the needs of all his people because he is God all-sufficient. He can do it all by himself because he is God, and nothing is too hard for the Lord.

A great supply

'My God shall supply all your need according to his riches in glory.' Not 'out of' his riches, but 'according to his riches'. What a great reservoir out of which this supply comes. What mortal can declare the riches of God's glory? The riches of his glory certainly takes in the riches of all creation (Psalm 50:10; Haggai 2:8), the riches of all providence (Romans 8:28; 11:36), and the riches of his grace (Ephesians 3:8). When we needed pardon, he washed us and made us whiter than snow in the blood of his Son. When we were naked, he brought forth the best robe, the righteousness of Christ, and put it on us!

'His riches in glory' go beyond what he has done. This reaches to what he can do. These riches include the riches of his infinite being. Who can calculate the possibilities of infinity and omnipotence? Yet, my God shall supply all your need according to all the infinite possibilities of his infinite Being!

God gives to the needs of his people consistent with his glory (Luke 11:9-13). God supplies our needs so as to bring glory to his name. God supplies the needs of his children in glorious ways. God supplies our needs in glorious measure. The Lord gives enough. He gives enough to all his people, enough of all we need, and enough for all time. We have numerous examples of the way God provides for his own in the Word of God. He fed the children of Israel with manna from heaven. He provided them with water from the rock. God's prophets were fed from Ahab's table. God commanded a raven to feed the prophet Elijah. There is nothing the mighty God cannot do and cannot supply.

177

A Great Mediator
Jesus Christ is the great mediator through whom all our needs are supplied by our God. 'My God shall supply all your need according to his riches in glory by Christ Jesus.' When God gives us Christ Jesus, he virtually gives us all things in Christ (Ephesians 1:3; Romans 8:32). God gives us all things through the merits of Christ. Jesus is our Joseph who opens all the storehouses of God's goodness, mercy and love (Genesis 41:56; John 17:1, 2). We must come to God through Christ and look to him for all things. God supplies your needs and mine for Christ's sake, through Christ's mediation, and by Christ's power.

If you are one of God's own dear children, one whose heart the Lord has renewed, take this promise of God, live upon it, rejoice, and give thanks. 'My God shall supply all your need according to his riches in glory by Christ Jesus.'

Index Of Bible Verses

Old Testament

Genesis
3:15   65
17:9-11   100
22:14   143
32:10   157
41:56   178

Exodus
20:4, 5   102
33:14   150

Deuteronomy
23:18   94

1 Samuel
2:30   176
3:18   143
12:23, 24   17
16:7   96, 101

2 Samuel
12:13   143
12:23   143
23:5   143

1 Chronicles
29:15   33

Nehemiah
8:10   93

Job
1:20-22   143
2:9, 10   143
5:7   56

7:6, 7   33
8:9   34
9:25, 26   34
14:1   56
14:1, 2   34
19:25-27   130
22:21   149
40:3-5   116
42:5, 6   116

Psalms
2:6-8   71
5:11   135
13:5, 6   137
16:10, 11   25
16:11   116
17:15   25, 104, 115, 116
23:1   149, 174
32:1, 2   136
32:11   135
34:1-7   102
34:10   174
34:14   149
34:19   175
37:1-8   144
37:23-25   174
37:24   175
40:7, 8   65
40:16   135
42:11   134
50:10   177
51:1-5   116
51:17   10
68:3   135

New Testament

Hebrews
1:1-3   64, 73, 136, 177
1:1-10 177
1:1-13 71
2:14, 15 37
2:17   65
4:3, 8, 10 149
4:12   100
4:15   72
4:16   144, 151, 159
5:7   65
5:8   65
5:8, 9 72
6:20   129
7:21-25 103
8:1   103
8:10-12 24
9:11, 12 103
9:12   48, 111
9:12-14 148
9:20   103
9:22   103
9:26   48, 111
10:5-14 71
10:11-14 96
10:16, 17 24
11:8-10 128
11:16 128
12:1-4 114
12:2   115
12:5-11 158
12:12-17 114
13:5   156, 176
13:7   19, 87, 171
13:10 102
13:13 53
13:17 19, 87, 171

James
2:14-20 79
4:3   151
4:10   72
4:14   34
4:17   83

1 Peter
1:3   111
1:4, 5 164
2:5   163
2:20-24 53
3:3, 4 43
3:18   66
4:11   19
4:13   53
4:14   53
5:7   149

2 Peter
2:1-3 92
5:13   72

1 John
1:9   122, 175
2:1, 2 103, 175
2:19   22
3:1   128, 129
3:1-5 149
3:2   131
3:2, 3 115
3:5   123
4:1   12, 92
4:4   166
5:1-3 82
5:7   64

Revelation
14:4   36
19:1-6 75
20:1-3 21

www.ingramcontent.com/pod-product-compliance
Lightning Source LLC
Chambersburg PA
CBHW020456100426
42812CB00024B/2674